W. S. Weeden

Peacemaker

A collection of sacred songs and hymns for use in all services of the church, Sunday school, home circle

W. S. Weeden

Peacemaker
A collection of sacred songs and hymns for use in all services of the church, Sunday school, home circle

ISBN/EAN: 9783337223045

Printed in Europe, USA, Canada, Australia, Japan

Cover: Foto ©Lupo / pixelio.de

More available books at **www.hansebooks.com**

THE PEACEMAKER

A COLLECTION OF SACRED SONGS AND HYMNS FOR USE IN ALL SERVICES OF THE CHURCH, SUNDAY-SCHOOL, HOME CIRCLE AND ALL KINDS OF EVANGELISTIC WORK. . . . .

EDITED BY

W. S. WEEDEN AND GEO. BEAVERSON.

PUBLISHED BY

WEEDEN & VAN DE VENTER,

NEW YORK: PITTSBURG, PA.:

W. S. WEEDEN, 149 FIFTH AVENUE.   J. W. VAN DE VENTER, 805-806 LEWIS BLOCK.

PREFACE.

No one can estimate the power of Christian song. Who will measure the influence of the hymns of apostolic times, the chants of Gregory, or the lyrics of Isaac Watts and Charles Wesley? In the great revivals of recent years gospel hymns have been hardly less potent than the preaching of our most effective evangelists. This new collection of Christian songs ought to find a hearty welcome. The authors have made their selections with greatest care. Hail to "**The Peacemaker!**" The glad words of the angel ring in our ears as we open this book—"On earth peace." The name is a good one. All the songs in the collection center about and exalt the life and character of the "**Prince of Peacemakers.**" Book of song, go thou to tens of thousands, carrying thy message of peace.

WILLIAM W. CRAWFORD,
President Allegheny College.

MEADVILLE, Pa., Aug. 25, 1894.

Blessed *are* the *Peacemakers:* for they shall be called the children of God.
MATT. V. 9.

NOTICE.

The words and music of nearly every piece in this book are copyright property, and cannot be reprinted in any form whatever without the written permission of the owners.
THE PUBLISHERS.

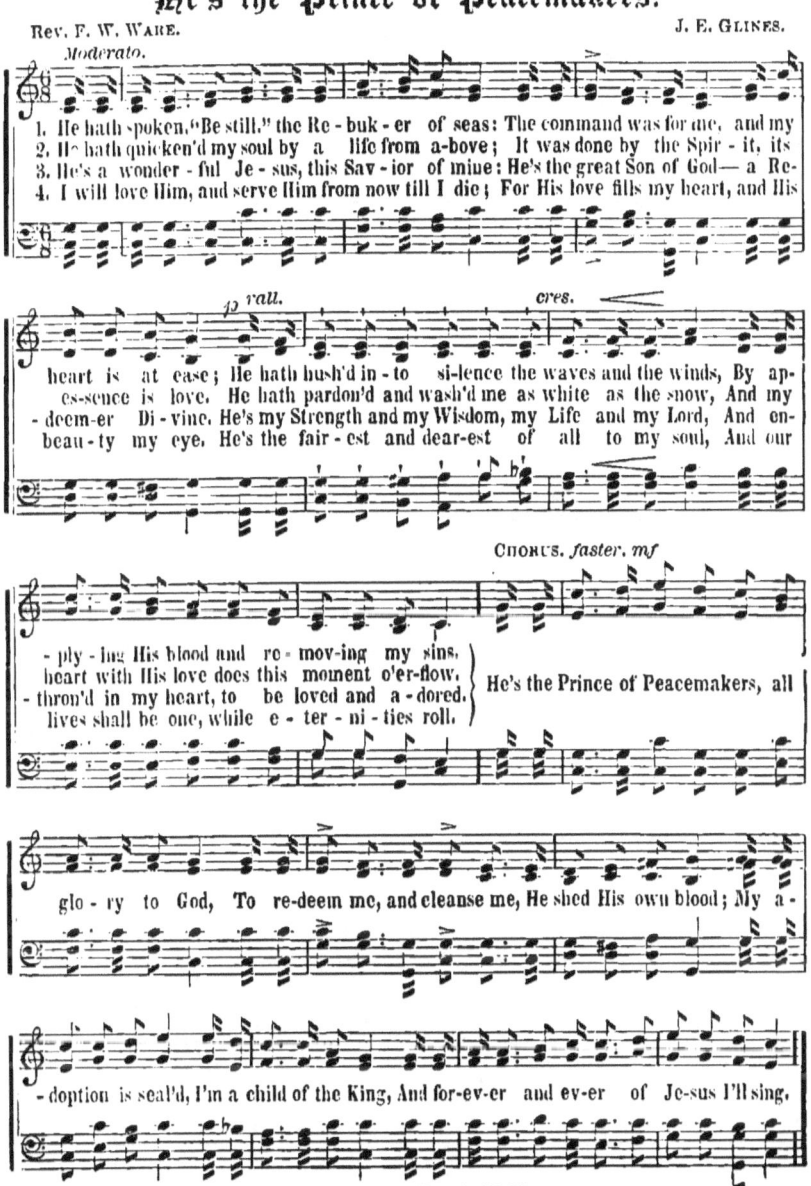

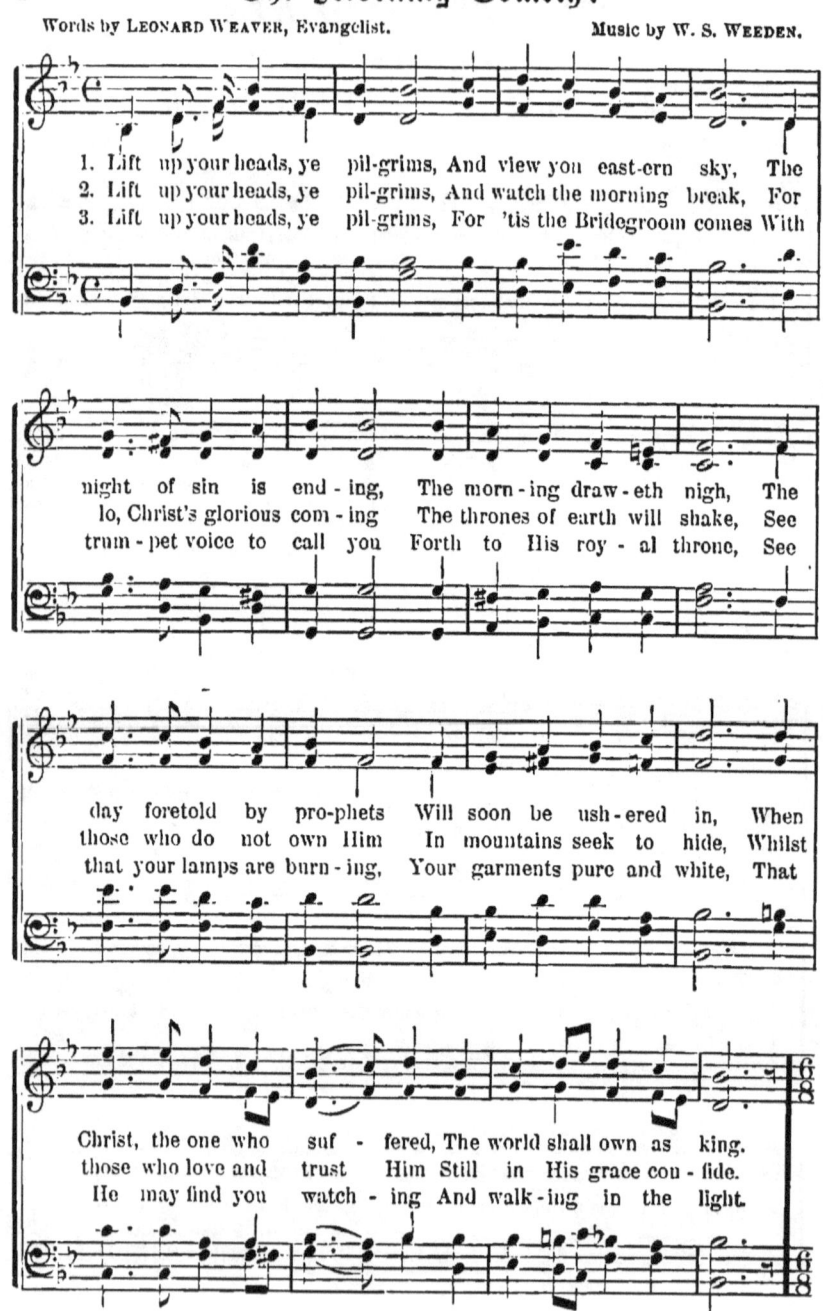

The Morning Cometh! Concluded.

He's com-ing by and by, He's com-ing by and by, The night of sin is end-ing, The morn-ing draw-eth nigh; He's com-ing by and by, He's com-ing by and by The night of sin is end-ing, The morn-ing draw-eth nigh.

4 Lift up your heads, ye pilgrims,
   And as ye journey on,
  Let Faith and Hope with courage
   Be ever firm and strong;
  Show by each word and action
   That Christ is real to you,
  And that His glorious coming
   Is ever clear in view.

5 Lift up your heads, ye pilgrims,
   Sing in that gladsome day,
  Nought but the Saviour's coming
   The tide of sin can stay.
  Creation groans whilst burdened
   For pain and toil to cease;
  Come, Prince of Life and Glory,
   Bring universal peace,

Oh! the Blood.

LEONARD WEAVER, Evangelist. W. S. WEEDEN.

1. When Jehovah pass'd thro' Egypt, the first-born there to slay, He told His servant Moses how the judgment he could stay; He gave to him a token true, the blood upon the door, And promised when He saw the blood the angel should pass o'er.
2. So Moses gath-ered Israel, and gave the Lord's command, And bid each for his own household secure a spotless Lamb, Then take its life and catch the blood and sprinkle on the door; And thus be saved from judgment when the angel should pass o'er.
3. They were saved from condemnation, when sheltered by the blood; 'Twas it alone on that dread night secured their peace with God; So thro' the blood of Christ my Lord, I have abiding peace, And from the bonds of sin and guilt a full and free release.
4. They are promised full salvation, who have this blood applied, And rest in faith upon the Lord who hath for sinners died; Come, sinners, get behind the blood, and know your sin forgiv'n; Then sing of grace which makes you meet to live with Him in heav'n.

CHORUS.

Oh! the blood, the precious blood, I trust in it to-day, The blood of Christ, the Lamb of God, takes all my sin away.

Copyright, 1894, by W. S. Weeden.

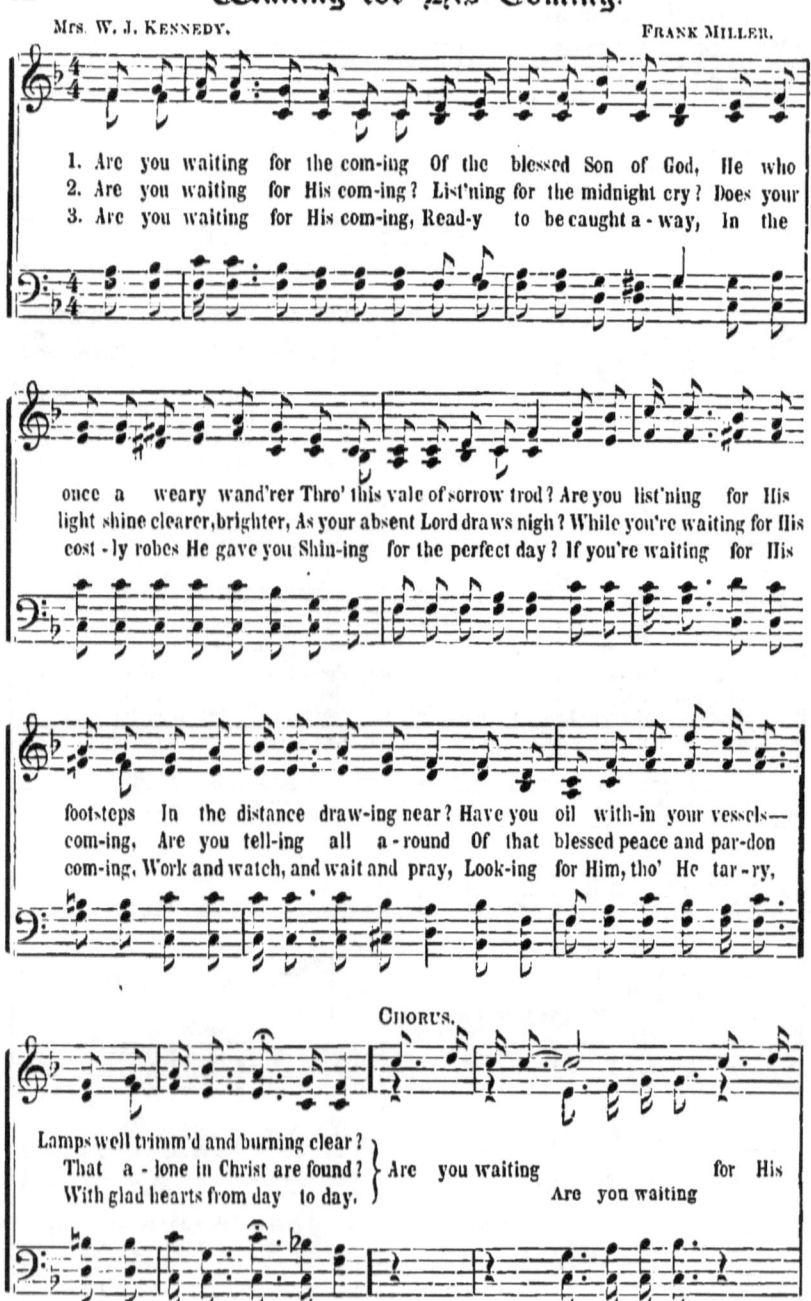

Waiting for His Coming. Concluded.

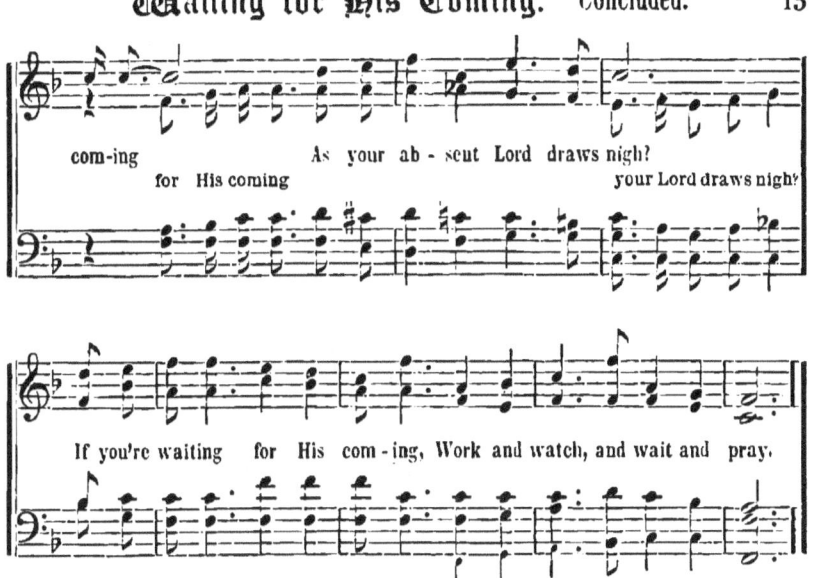

Begin the Day with God.

FRANK MILLER.

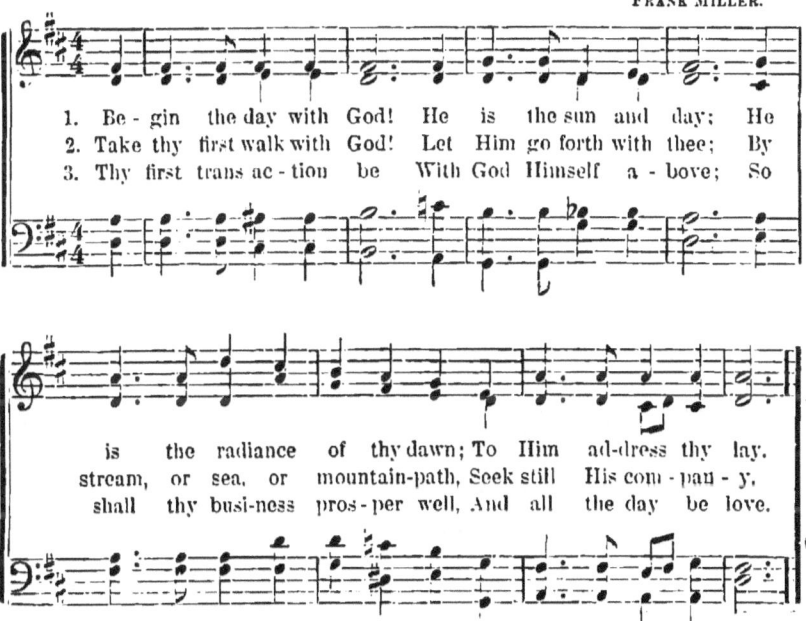

1. Be-gin the day with God! He is the sun and day; He is the radiance of thy dawn; To Him ad-dress thy lay.
2. Take thy first walk with God! Let Him go forth with thee; By stream, or sea, or mountain-path, Seek still His com-pan-y,
3. Thy first trans ac - tion be With God Himself a - bove; So shall thy busi-ness pros-per well, And all the day be love.

Copyright, 1894, by Frank Miller.

Sought and Found. Concluded.

Jesus the Reconciler.

"God was in Christ, reconciling the world unto himself."

ALICE CARY.   PHILIP PHILLIPS, Jr.

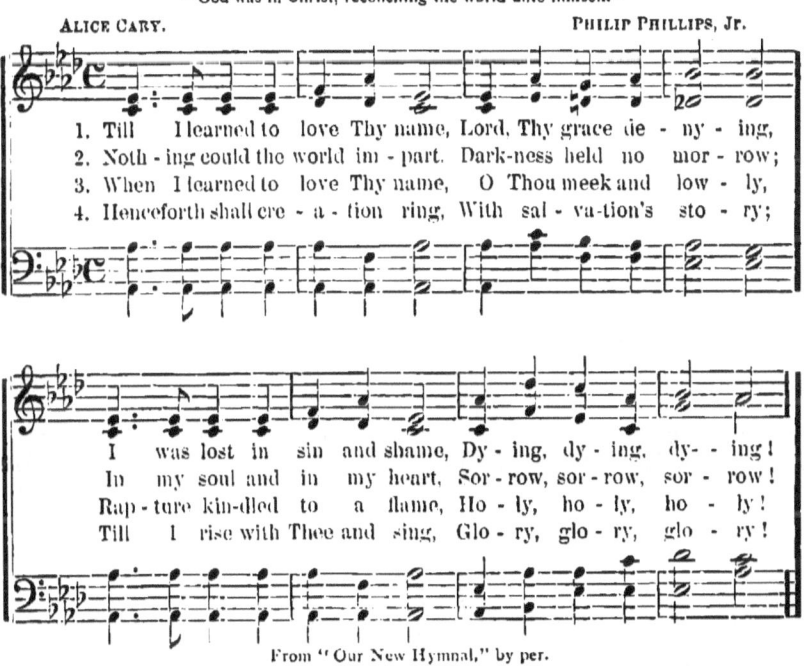

From "Our New Hymnal," by per.

Only a Word.

1. On-ly a word for the Master, Lov-ing-ly, qui-et-ly, said,
2. On-ly a word of re-monstrance, Sor-row-ful, gen-tle, and deep;
3. On-ly some act of de-vo-tion, Will-ing-ly, joy-ful-ly done;

On-ly a word, Yet the Master heard, And some fainting hearts were fed.
On-ly a look, Yet the strong man shook, And he went a-lone to weep.
"Surely 'twas naught,"—So the proud world tho't,—Yet souls for Christ are won.

REFRAIN.
On-ly a word, on-ly a word, On-ly a word for the Mast-er;
On-ly a word, on-ly a word, On-ly a word for the Mas-ter.

4 Only an hour for the children,
Pleasantly, cheerfully given;
Seed was there sown,
In that hour alone,
Which would bring forth fruit for heav'n.

5 "Only"—but Jesus is looking
Constantly, tenderly down,
Earthward, and sees
Those who strive to please,
And their love loves to crown.

18. Christian, how can You Stand Waiting.

LEONARD WEAVER, Evangelist.   W. S. WEEDEN.

1. Christian, how can you stand wait-ing For some work to do,
   When the Mas-ter now is call-ing, Call-ing un-to you?
   Go and work to-day, my broth-er, In the harv-est field;
   See, the gold-en grain is read-y—Now thy sick-le wield.

2. Un-to you the Sav-ior giv-eth Peace and joy and rest,
   Canst thou tar-ry with-out knowing Oth-ers, too, are blest?
   How canst thou with-hold the tid-ings Of the Sav-ior's love,
   All the bless-ed gos-pel message Of the Son of God.

3. Gath-er lit-tle children 'round you, As He did of old,
   Tell them how the Shepherd gath-ers Lambs un-to His fold;
   And that they may come and trust Him For pro-tect-ing care,
   That He'll guide them ev-er on-ward, All His grace to share.

Copyright, 1894, by W. S. Weeden.

Christian, how can You, etc. Concluded.

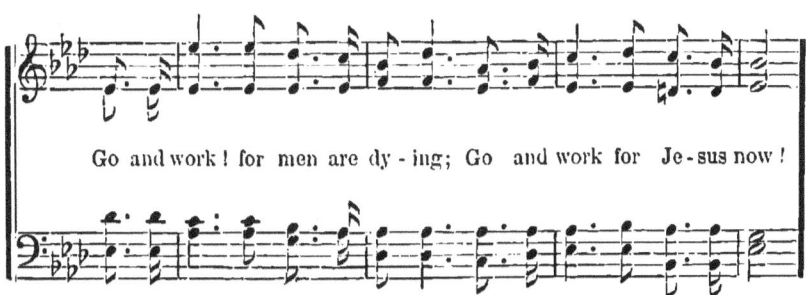

4
Go then to the old and wrinkled,
  With their years of sin;
Tell them how they may be pardoned,
  And Salvation win.
Go to all, make no exception,
  Bid them seek His face;
For the world may come and prove Him,
  And receive His grace.

5
Many wandering on in darkness
  Long to know the way
From their sin, and pain, and sorrow,
  To the realms of day.
Take the gospel of Salvation,
  Make it known to all;
Pray and plead until believing
  On His name they call.

Phelps.

Words and Music by PHILIP PHILLIPS, Jr.

1. A guilt-y sin-ner once was I, Till God in heaven heard my cry;
2. I can-not tell His love to thee. I on-ly know He died for me,—
3. The pass-ing days their tri-als bring, Yet thro' them all His ac-cents ring,

And bade me at my Savior's feet, Find rest and hap-pi-ness com-plete.
And that because by faith I cried I found, for ne'er was faith denied.
"Come un-to me, and com-ing rest," And each new blessing seems the best.

There as I caught His look of love He wrote my name in heav'n a-bove
A-lone I went to Him, and there He made me His— O vis-ion fair!
The seasons come, the seasons go, But He a-bideth true, I know,

And ev-er since my song has been, All-glo-ry to my Sav-ior King!
His great for-giv-ing love to see And know He died for me, for me!
Who bore my sins on Cal-va-ry, And changing not, still lov-eth me!

CHORUS.

Je-sus, Sav-ior, Thy dy-ing blood wash-es white in its cleansing flood;

Copyright, 1894, by Philip Phillips, Jr.

Phelps. Concluded.

To that fountain my sins I bring, Glo-ry to my Sav-ior King!

An Evening Prayer.

"C." FRANK MILLER.

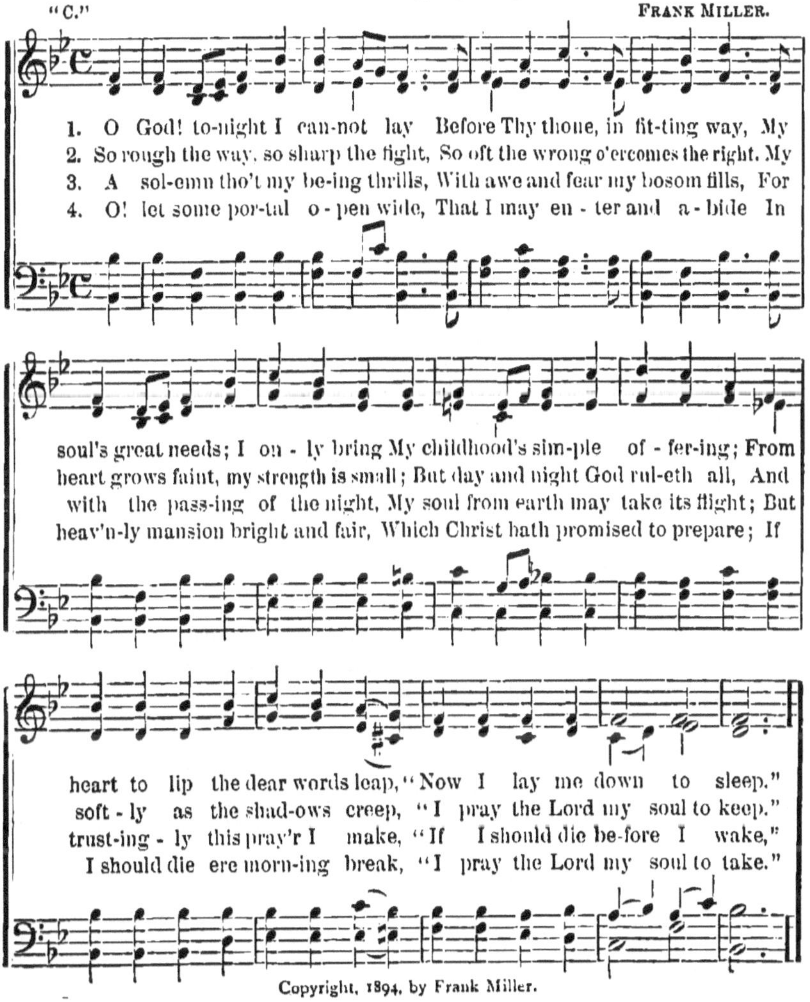

1. O God! to-night I can-not lay Before Thy throne, in fit-ting way, My
2. So rough the way, so sharp the fight, So oft the wrong o'ercomes the right. My
3. A sol-emn tho't my be-ing thrills, With awe and fear my bosom fills, For
4. O! let some por-tal o-pen wide, That I may en-ter and a-bide In

soul's great needs; I on-ly bring My childhood's sim-ple of-fer-ing; From
heart grows faint, my strength is small; But day and night God rul-eth all, And
with the pass-ing of the night, My soul from earth may take its flight; But
heav'n-ly mansion bright and fair, Which Christ hath promised to prepare; If

heart to lip the dear words leap, "Now I lay me down to sleep."
soft-ly as the shad-ows creep, "I pray the Lord my soul to keep."
trust-ing-ly this pray'r I make, "If I should die be-fore I wake,"
I should die ere morn-ing break, "I pray the Lord my soul to take."

Copyright, 1894, by Frank Miller.

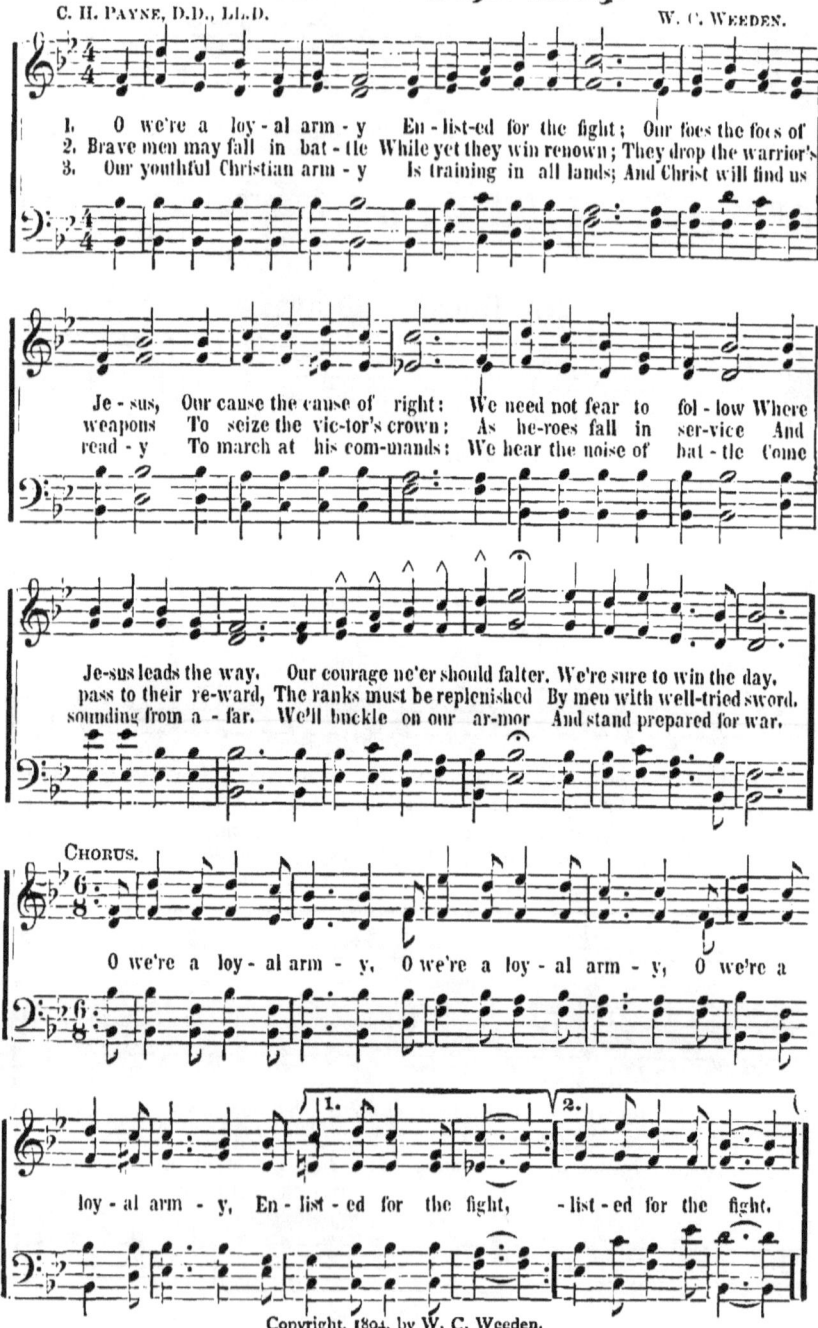

26. Oh! that I Knew.

LEONARD WEAVER, Evangelist.   W. S. WEEDEN.

1. Oh! that I knew where I might find The One who saves from sin, To free my soul and make me whole That I might live for Him.
2. Oh! that I knew where I might find The nev-er-fail-ing Friend, Who nev-er leaves, but ev-er cleaves, And keeps un-to the end.
3. Oh! that I knew where I might find The Christ that sat-is-fies, With heav'n-ly rest up-on His breast, And ev'-ry need sup-plies.
4. Blest Savior, help me seek and find, Oh! bid me not de-part, I will be-lieve, and now re-ceive Thy love in-to my heart.

CHORUS.

Thank God thou hast not far to go, For He is ev-er near, And if you seek Him you will find, And feel His presence here. Thank God thou hast not far to go, For He is ev-er near, And

Copyright, 1894, by W. S. Weeden.

Oh! that I Knew. Concluded.

if you seek Him you will find, And feel His presence here.

Come, Sinner, Come.

WILL. E. WITTER.   H. R. PALMER. By per.

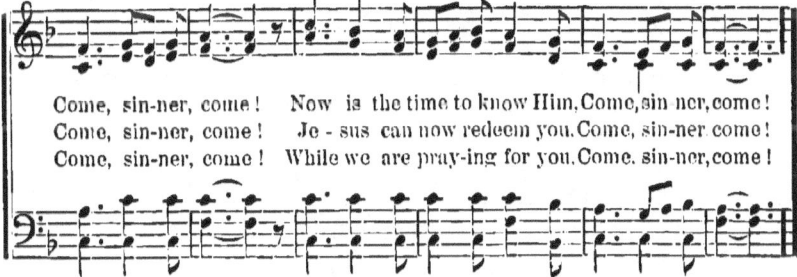

1. While Jesus whispers to you, Come, sinner, come! While we are praying for you, Come, sinner, come! Now is the time to own Him, Come, sinner, come! Now is the time to know Him, Come, sinner, come!
2. Are you too heavy laden? Come, sinner, come! Jesus will bear your burden, Come, sinner, come! Jesus will not deceive you, Come, sinner, come! Jesus can now redeem you, Come, sinner come!
3. Oh, hear his tender pleading, Come, sinner, come! Come and receive the blessing, Come, sinner, come! While Jesus whispers to you, Come, sinner, come! While we are praying for you, Come, sinner, come!

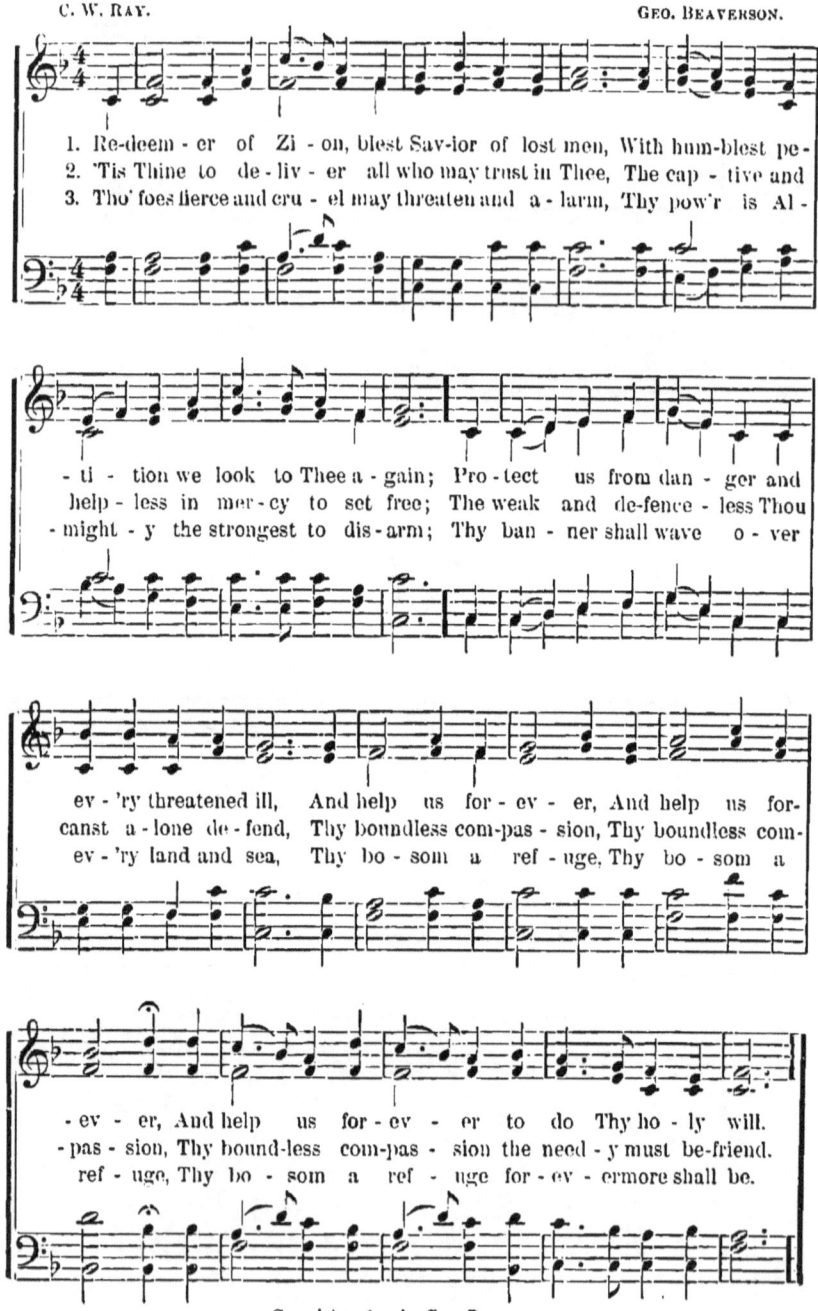

Listen to My Story.

J. W. VAN DE VENTER. S. C. FOSTER, Arr.

1. Down at the cross the Savior found me, Weary of sin;
   Then Jesus saw me, weak and weary, Came to my soul;
   Darkness was ev'ry-where around me, Sorrow and gloom within.
   Brought sunshine to my heart so dreary, Whisper'd, and I was whole.

CHORUS.
Listen, listen to my story: At His feet I bow;
He saves me, and He keeps me—glory! Praise the Lord! He saves me now!

2. He found me on a barren mountain,
   Hungry and cold;
   He bro't me to the cleansing fountain,
   Placed me within the fold;
   I know the Savior will protect me,
   Show me the way;
   He never, never will neglect me,
   I shall not go astray.

3. He fills my heart to overflowing—
   Wonderful love!
   Rich blessings He is now bestowing,
   Peace from the throne above.
   Now when temptations great assail me,
   I can endure;
   His grace and mercy never fail me,
   He makes His child secure.

Copyright, 1894, by J. W. Van De Venter.

Christ Victorious.

EVALYN COUARD, Deaconess,
New York City.

KATE O. CURTS, Deaconess,
New York City.

Moderato.

1. Walking dai - ly with the Master, List'ning hour - ly to His voice;
2. Lift - ing bur - dens for our neighbors That are great - er than our own,
3. Trusting quiet - ly in as - sur-ance That our Mas - ter doth partake

Helping Him.. His sheaves to gather—In His work.. our hearts rejoice.
Helping those.. who faint around us To ap - proach the roy-al throne.
Of our tri - als and our triumphs; We shall win... for "Jesus' sake."

CHORUS.
Marcato.

Christ vic - to - rious! oh, the glo - ry Of the glad tri - umph-ant song—

When the na - tions learn the sto - ry And to Je - sus Christ be - long.

Copyright, 1894, by W. S. Weeden.

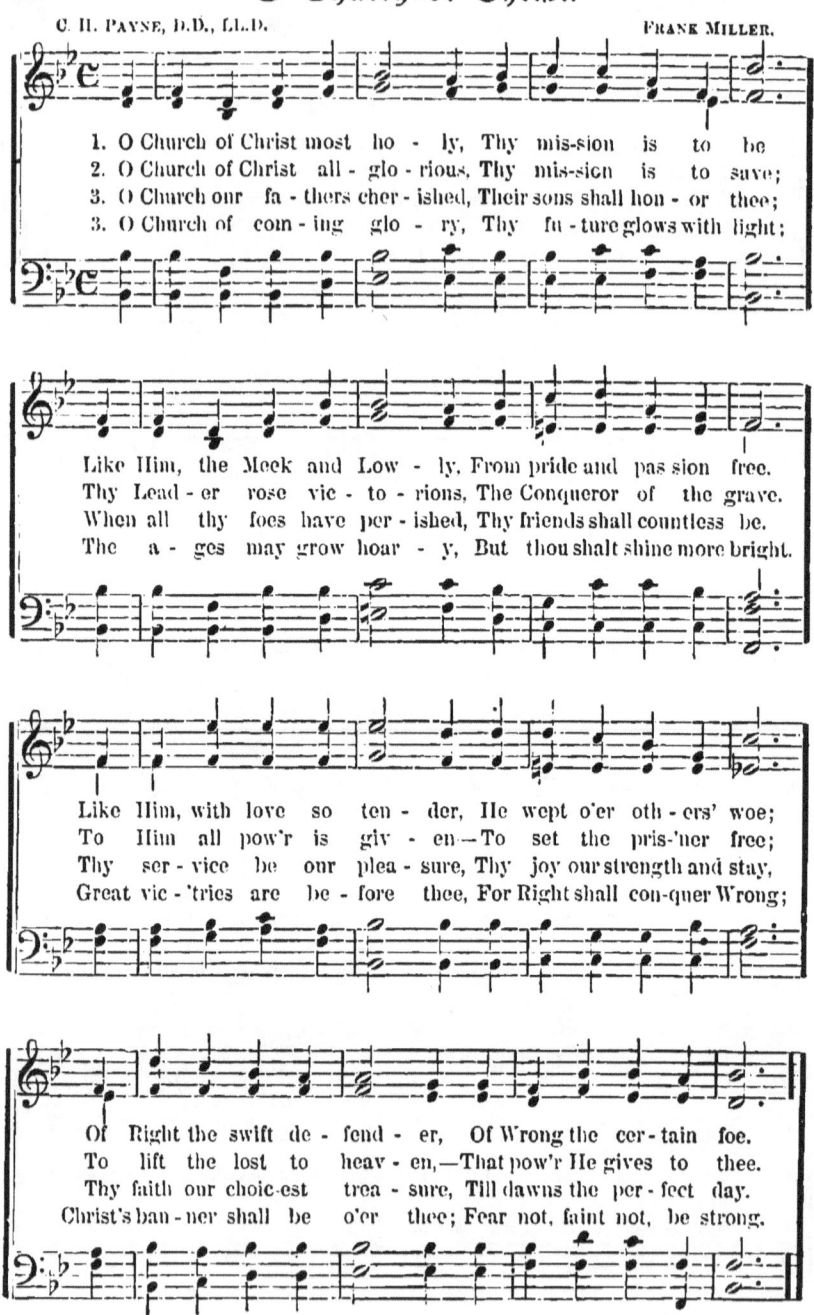

Let Me Die at My Post.

Lines written by Wm. Hunter, D.D., on the death of Rev. Gideon D. Kinnear, while preaching at Hollow Rock Campmeeting on the evening of September 5th, 1875. Near the close of his discourse he was observed to stagger; some persons ran to his assistance. Feeling that he was failing, he said, "Let the meeting go on; let me die at my post;" and the very last words he uttered were, "All is well." He immediately became unconscious and remained so until death.

W. HUNTER D.D.   J. HARRY HORNER.

1. An old sol-dier I stand with my sword in my hand, Till I catch the glad summons di-vine; Lo! the sig-nal I see, He is com-ing for me; All is well!.... I am His, He is mine.
2. Let the meet-ing go on! I will short-ly be gone; Let an-oth-er the mes-sage re-peat; In the blood that was shed there is life from the dead; O ye ransomed, come, bow at His feet.
3. Let the meet-ing go on! when the conquest is won, And the Lord from the o-pen-ing skies, Shall in glo-ry come down, with the long-promised crown, All the sleep-ers in Christ shall a-rise.
4. When He com-eth to reign we shall come in His train, To His saints shall the kingdom be giv'n; With our last la-bor done and our last bat-tle won, We shall shine.... as the stars in the heav'ns.

CHORUS.

Let the meeting go on! Let me die at my post! Let me fall in the van of the con-quer-ing host; Let the meeting go

Copyright, 1894, by W. S. Weeden.

Let Me Die at My Post. Concluded.

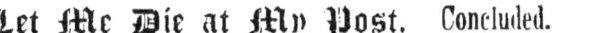

on! Let me die at my post! All is well! All is well!

How They Crucified My Lord.
(JUBILEE SONG) Arr. by M. E. BLISS-WILLSON.

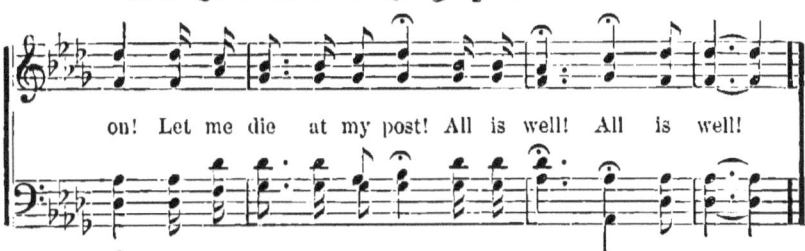

1. When I think how they cru-ci-fied my Lord, When I cru-ci-fied my Lord, think how they crucified my Lord, Oh, sometimes it causes me to think how they cru-ci-fied my Lord, tremble, tremble, tremble, When I think how they cru-ci-fied my Lord.

2. When I think how they crowned Him with the thorns.
3. When I think how they nailed Him to the tree.
4. When I think how they pierced Him in the side.
5. When I think how they laid Him in the tomb.
6. When I think how the stone was rolled away.
7. When I think how He rose up from the grave.

Used by permission.

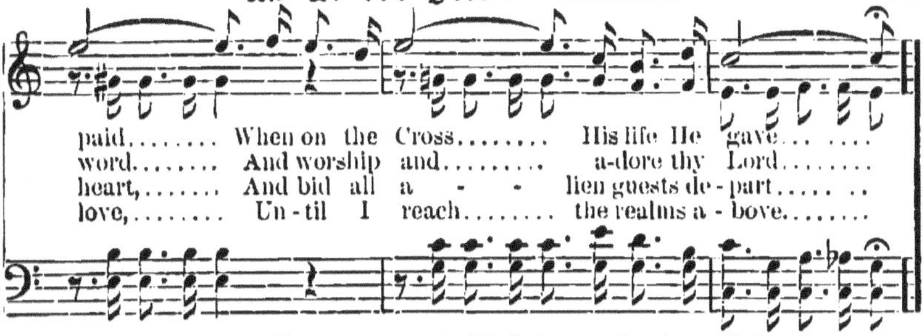

Is It for Me? Concluded. 45

paid....... When on the Cross........ His life He gave......
word........ And worship and......... a-dore thy Lord........
heart,....... And bid all a - - lien guests de - part...... ..
love,........ Un - til I reach........ the realms a - bove........

5 Is it for me he soon will come,
When He shall call His people home?
Shall I then hear the trumpet voice?
Will it make my poor heart rejoice?
It is for me He soon will come
To take me to His home above;
Then in the twinkling of an eye
I'll rise to meet Him in the sky.

6 Oh, help me, Lord, until that day,
To faithful keep and never stray;
To live for Thee from morn till night,
And find in Thee my soul's delight.
So shall I praise Thy glorious name,
And spread abroad Thy wondrous fame;
And others by my life shall see
That Thou art all in all to me.

HENRIETTA LAWTON FISHER. **We are Thine.** GEO. BEAVERSON.

Moderato.

1. Precious Sa - vior, we are Thine, Thine by right and choice; Let Thy
2. Precious Sa - vior, we are Thine; We have heard Thy voice Call - ing
3. Precious Sa - vior, we are Thine, Bought with won - drous price; May we

CHORUS.

love around us shine; Make our hearts re-joice.
gently, come, be mine, Make my yoke thy choice. } Precious Savior, we are Thine,
in Thy kingdom shine, With Thine own re - joice.

Thine in life to be; Precious Savior, we are Thine Thro' all e - ter - ni - ty.

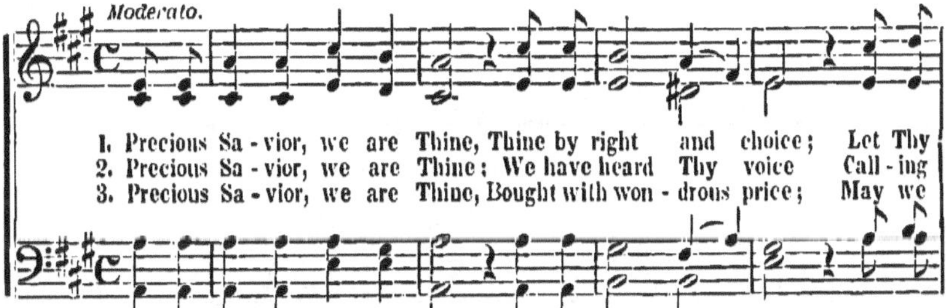

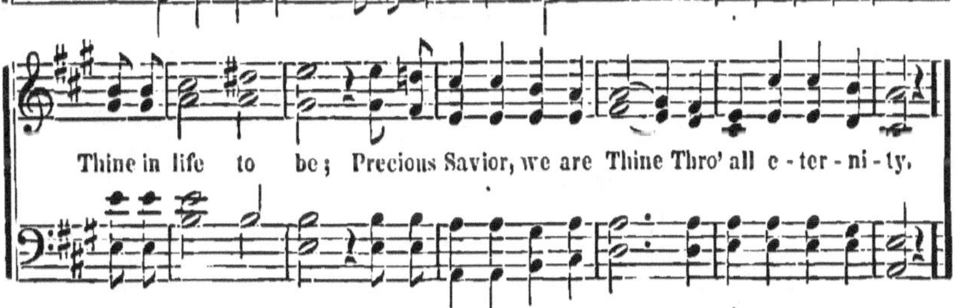

Copyright, 1894, by Geo. Beaverson.

Saved by His Blood. Concluded.

Hal-le-lu - jah! Hal-le-lu - jah! I am saved by His blood.
Hal-le-lu - jah! Hal-le-lu - jah!

Where will You Spend Eternity?

ELIZA SHERMAN. C. C. CASE.
SOLO OR DUET.

1. Where will you spend e - ter - ni - ty? Oh! child of love for whom Christ died,
2. Where will you spend e - ter - ni - ty? The King of Glo - ry bids thee come;
3. Where will you spend e - ter - ni - ty? Time's solemn bells soon cease to chime;

The harvest time will soon be gone, Oh! hast-en, hast-en to de-cide.
Ac - cept of Him and He will give A bright, e - ter - nal, glorious home.
God's spir-it will not always strive, Time's bell tolls on; be wise in time.

CHORUS.

E - ter - ni - ty! E - ter - ni - ty! Where will you spend e-
-ter - ni - ty? Where will you spend e - ter - ni - ty?

Copyright, 1891, by C. C. Case.

Precious Truth. Concluded.

hap - py cho-rus, Sing - ing, sing - ing, Our Savior's praise;
still the cho-rus, Tell - ing, tell - ing, His wondrous love;
-loud the cho-rus, Glo - ry, glo - ry, To God on high.

Singing, singing, singing, singing,
Tell-ing, tell-ing, tell-ing, tell-ing,
Glo-ry, glo-ry, glo-ry, glo-ry,

Jesus is Calling Now.

Rev. E. A. HOFFMAN.   GEO. BEAVERSON.

1. Je - sus is call-ing you now! Come to His arms of love; He will pre-
2. Je - sus is call-ing to - day,— Why will you long-er wait? Cast all your
3. Je - sus is call-ing to you; Pledge Him, in solemn vow, Spir - it, and

CHORUS.

-pare your soul   For the home a - bove ⎫
sins a - way,—   En - ter Mer-cy's gate. ⎬ Call-ing now, call-ing now,
life, and all,—   He will save you now! ⎭

Je-sus is call-ing now! At the cross hum-bly bow,—He will save you now!

Copyright, 1882, by John J. Hood.

Ring Out, Ye Gospel Bells. Concluded.

3.
Ring out, ring out, ye gospel bells,
  Your *solemn* tones prolong,
For in the broad and downward road,
  Amongst the careless throng,
Are those who oft your notes have heard,
  But still they disobey:
Plead with them tenderly yet warn:
  Now is Salvation's day.

4.
Ring out, ring out, ye gospel bells,
  Sometimes *in undertones*,
For lo! there comes from dying ones
  A sad and awful groan;
My life is past, oh, hear their cry,
  The harvest time gone by;
I've gained the world, but oh, the cost!
  My soul, my soul is lost!

56. Oh, Admit Him!

JACOB CRIST. W. S. WEEDEN.

1. Hear your blessed Mas-ter pleading, For ad-mission to your heart; Be not stub-born or un-heed-ing, Else from you He may de-part; Oh, ad-mit the great Phy-si-cian, Hast-en now to let Him in; Do not ren-der void His mis-sion—Your de-cep-tive heart to win.
2. Choose you now His free sal-va-tion, That you may be born a-new, Suf-fer not pro-cras-ti-na-tion To steal pre-cious time from you; Let Him in: He long has wait-ed, Stand-ing at the bolt-ed door, Bow to Him, whom once you hat-ed, Let Him stand with-out no more.
3. En-ter not the val-ley friendless, Let Him in—your need is great; His de-par-ture may be end-less, Fix-ing your e-ter-nal state. Hear your bless-ed Mas-ter plead-ing For ad-mis-sion to your heart; Be not stub-born or un-heed-ing, Else from you He may de-part.

CHORUS.

Oh, admit Him! Oh, admit Him! O-pen ere it be too late, ere it be too late.

Copyright, 1894, by W. S. Weeden.

Oh, Admit Him! Concluded.

His de-par-ture may be end-less, Fix-ing your e-ter-nal state.

The King's Highway.

"And an highway shall be there."—Isaiah xxxv: 8.

PRISCILLA J. OWENS.   CHAS. EDW. PRIOR.

With animation.

1. We're marching to Mount Zi-on,   We keep the King's highway;   We
2. When foes encamp a-round us,   We look to Christ and pray;   Tho'
3. We see the tow-ers shin-ing,   They bright-en day by day;   Our

CHORUS.

have a mighty Leader, We walk in white array. We're marching to Mount Zion, We
war should rise against us, We keep the King's highway.
home is drawing nearer, We sing up-on the way.

keep the King's highway; 'Tis blest to follow Jesus, Come, walk with us to-day.

Copyright, 1885, by Chas. Edw. Prior.

Little Things.

C. H. PAYNE, D.D., LL.D.
W. S. WEEDEN.

1. When you see a mighty forest, With its tall and sturdy trees,
2. When you gaze upon a mountain, With its proud, majestic form
3. When you see a stately temple, Fair and beautiful and bright,

Lifting up their giant branches; Wrestling with the wintry breeze;
Tow'ring upward to the heavens, All unshaken by the storm,
With its lofty tow'rs and turrets Glist'ning in the sun's clear light,

Do not fail to learn the lesson Which the moaning winds resound,
Then remember that the mountain Is built up of grains of sand,
Think how soon the noble structure Would to shapeless ruin fall,

Ev-'ry oak was once an acorn, All unnoticed on the ground.
Which an infant child might scatter With its tiny, feeble hand.
Were it not for sure foundations Firmly laid beneath it all.

4 When you see a goodly nation
   Strong and free and proud and great,
With its statesmen, scholars, poets,
   All its men of high estate,
Keep in mind that all these great ones,
   To whom honors high you pay,
Once were only little people,
   Children such as we to-day.

5 In the building of our temple,
   Noble temple of the state,
As a refuge of true freemen,
   Both the lowly and the great.
Do not slight the little builders,
   Let us have some humble place,
Lay with us the sure foundation,
   Then you'll shout the capstone's grace.

Copyright, 1894, by W. S. Weeden.

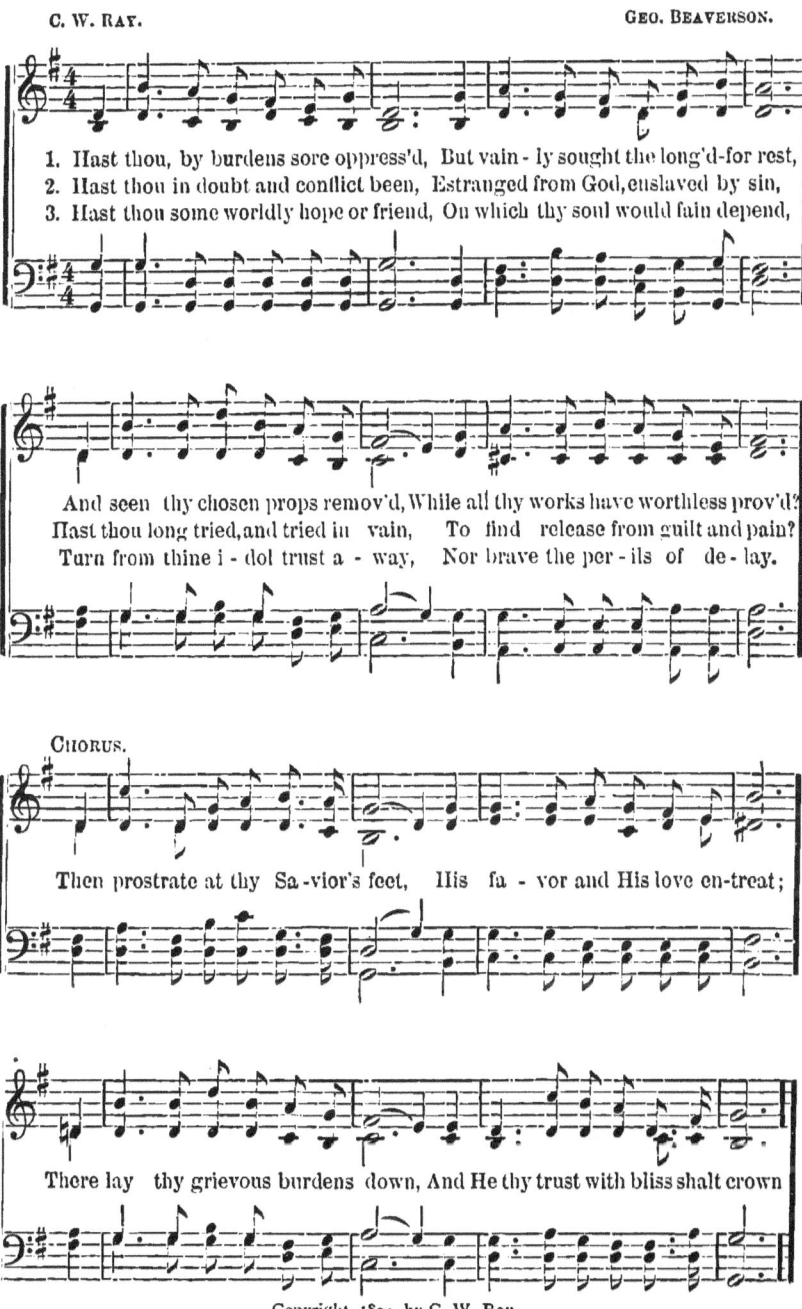

Our Loved Ones, Our Lost Ones.

SARAH J. C. WHITTLESEY.   J. HARRY HORNER.

1. They are safe in the har-bor, the white sails are furled, The an-chor is
2. How far from this earth-home, oh! where on the plane Of the pur-ple im-
3. A-way, far a-way, in the vi-o-let glow, A-cross the wide
4. Yes, here by the home-hearth with love-light-ed eyes, A breath of their

cast by the ev-ergreen shore: They are liv-ing to-geth-er in God's love-ly
-mense is the sweet ev-er-more: When af-ter life's sun-set we'll meet them a-
waste of a fath-om-less sea: Un-think-ing of us are they rest-ing, no,
presence drifts thro' the dim days: They come swift as tho't from their home in the

world, Our loved ones, our lost ones, they sor-row no more, They sor-row no
-gain, Our loved ones, our lost ones, who wait on the shore, Who wait on the
no! Our loved ones, our lost ones, are with you and me, Are with you and
skies, Our loved ones, our lost ones, they guard us al-ways, They guard us al-

more, They sor-row no more, Our loved ones, our lost ones, they sorrow no more.
shore, Who wait on the shore, Our loved ones, our lost ones, who wait on the shore.
me, Are with you and me, Our loved ones, our lost ones, are with you and me.
-ways, They guard us al-ways, Our loved ones, our lost ones, they guard us always.

5 I watch the long vacant old arm-chair sometimes,
   Soul-yearning to see them and hear them once more;
  I know it is vain, till the last vesper chimes,
   Our loved ones, our lost ones, we'll see them no more.

6 But oh! when the rose-tint of earth-life shall pale,
   And the mortal lies down with its sorrow and pain,
  And the freed spirit passes beyond the dim veil,
   Our loved ones, our lost ones, we'll meet them again.

Copyright, 1894, by W. S. Weeden.

5 Ring out, ring on, ye bells of trust,
For God hath said perform He must;
'Tis on His truth my all I stake,
No tempest-storms that Rock can shake.

6 Ring out, ring on, ye bells of heaven,
'Tis sweet to know all sin forgiven;
But oh, thy courts I soon shall see,
And share thy full felicity.

Copyright, 1894, by W. S. Weeden.

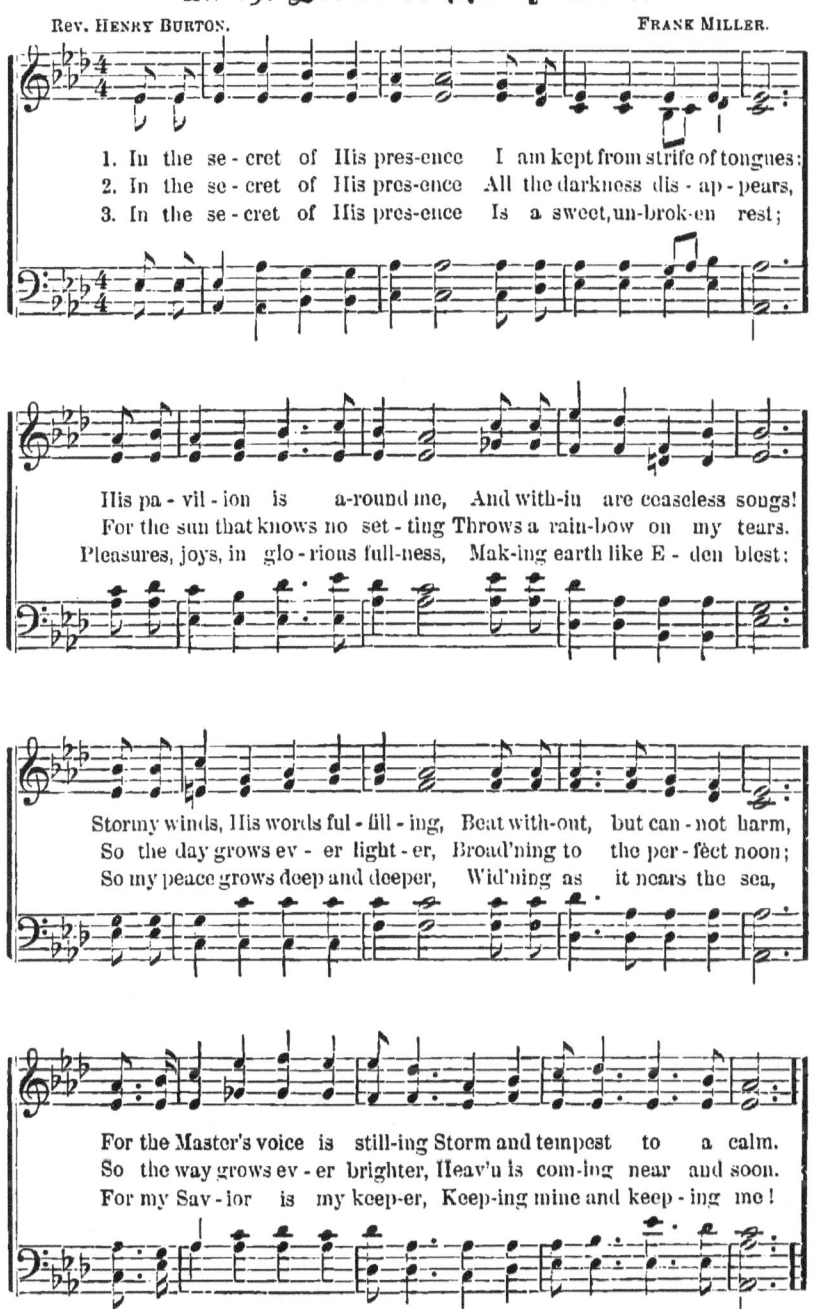

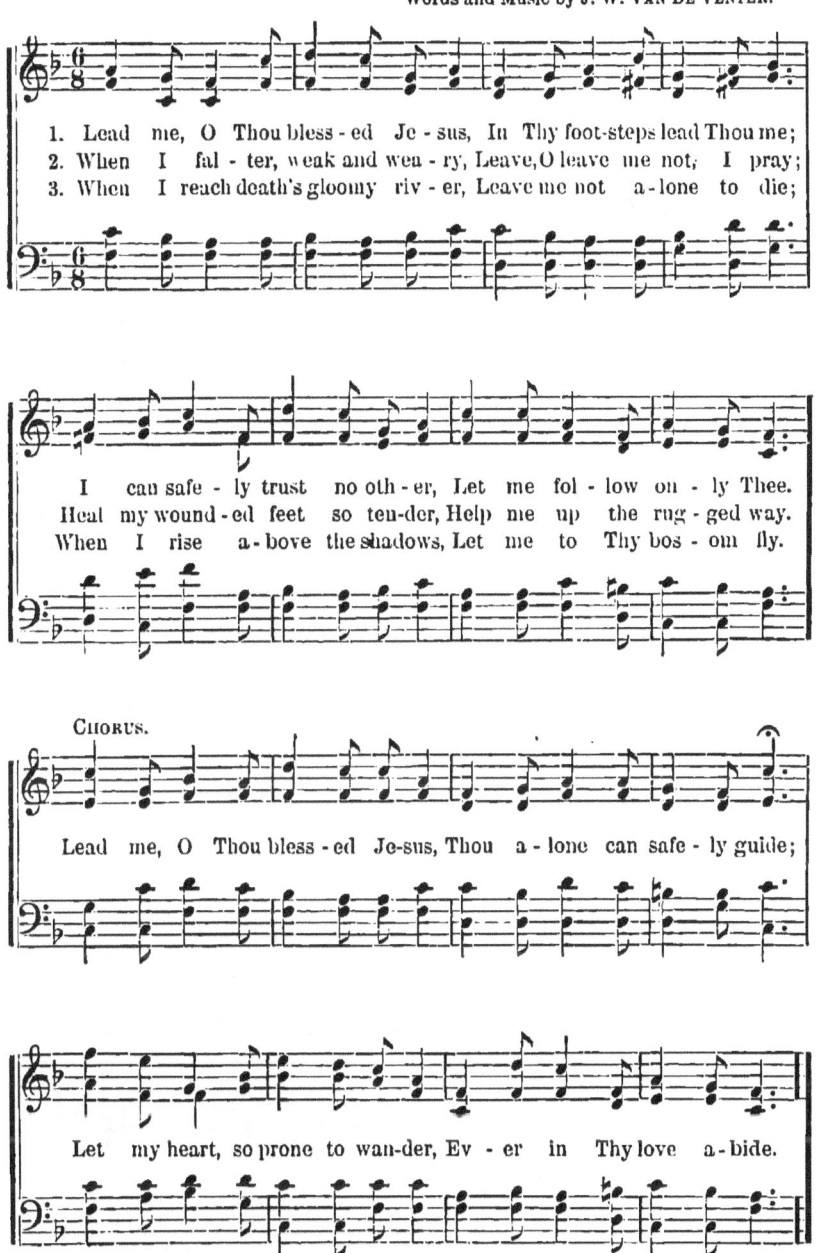

He Saves to the Uttermost. 73

FANNY J. CROSBY.   CARYL FLORIO.

1. Our blessed Redeemer came down from above To bring us good tidings of wonderful love; Then listen with gladness, His message receive:—He saves to the uttermost all who believe.
2. Behold, He is calling! No longer delay; His arms are extended in mercy to-day; He waits to be gracious, your souls to receive:—He saves to the uttermost all who believe.
3. Come hither, ye thirsty, where'er you may be, Life's waters are flowing, salvation is free; O come without money, full pardon receive:—He saves to the uttermost all who believe.
4. O come to the banquet prepared for the world, And rest 'neath His standard so widely unfurl'd; There's room, and the welcome that all may receive:—He saves to the uttermost all who believe.

REFRAIN.
He saves to the uttermost, Saves to the uttermost, Saves to the uttermost All who believe.

Copyright, 1894, by S. M. Bixby. Used by permission.

My Mother's Silv'ry Hair. Concluded. 75

Published in Sheet Music form, price 40 cents per copy.

The Daily Cross.

"If any man will come after me, let him deny himself, and take up his cross, and follow me."—Matt. 16: 24.

JAS. H. ROBINSON.

1. Who fain would fol-low Je-sus, A dai-ly cross must bear;
2. Who fain would fol-low Je-sus, The Mas-ter's life must heed;
3. Who fain would fol-low Je-sus, He can-not step a-side
4. Who fain would fol-low Je-sus, Thro' strife, and shame, and death,

With nev-er-ceas-ing pa-tience, With watch-ful-ness and prayer;
Must spend him-self for oth-ers, And hear when oth-ers plead;
Scorn-ing the weak and tempted, In loft-i-ness of pride.
Will sit with Him in glo-ry— This the Mes-si-ah saith.

And, morn-ing af-ter morn-ing, Must tread the up-ward way,
Must ev-er bear the fall-en In arms of bless-ing up,
For who would fol-low Je-sus, Must min-gle in the throng,
The dai-ly cross, my broth-er, And then the crown and palm;

That leads thro' pain and con-flict To love's e-ter-nal day.
And oft to lips in sor-row, Hold sweet compassion's cup.
And aid when hun-ger wail-eth, And stoop to right the wrong.
Here lost and ma-ny-a tri-al; There heav'n's un-end-ing psalm.

Copyright, 1894, by W. S. Weeden.

82. The Pharisee and Publican.

LEONARD WEAVER, Evangelist.   W. S. WEEDEN.

1. There went to the tem-ple to of-fer up prayer, A Pub-li-can and Phar-i-see bold; And you who are hop-ing by works to be saved, Pray list to the sto-ry so old. The Phar-i-see stood and prayed with him-self And glo-ried in what he had done; As if by his mer-it he

2. The Pub-li-can stood and smote on his breast, Not dar-ing to look to the sky, For he felt his con-di-tion and owned with contrition, No mer-it had he to come nigh. Have mer-cy, O God! on a sin-ner like me, This alone was the cry of his heart; Whilst the Phar-i-see wondered why

3. The Pub-li-can's prayer for mer-cy was heard, He was blest and for-giv-en that day; Whilst he who came boasting received not the blessing, De-ceived he went emp-ty a-way. Then trust not your goodness to save you from sin, Plead on-ly God's mer-cy so free; And then you be-liev-ing, His

Copyright, 1894, by W. S. Weeden.

The Pharisee and Publican. Concluded.

CHORUS.

thought to in-her-it A place in the heav'n-ly home,
God did not bid, The Pub-li-can sin-ner de-part.
fa-vor re-ceiv-ing, The glo-ries of heav'n shall see.
It's not by my working, it's not by my praying, Sal-va-tion from sin can be won; It is by be-liev-ing, It is by re-ceiv-ing, I'm saved thro' faith in God's Son.

The Lord's Prayer.

Matt vi.  GREGORIAN.

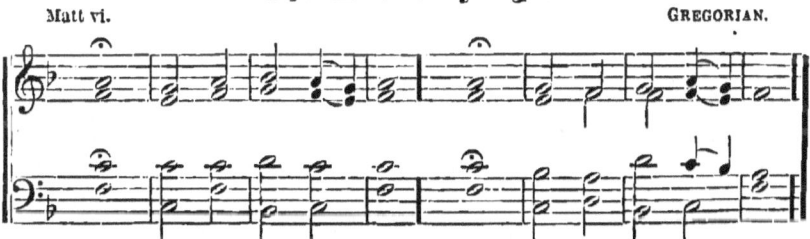

1. Our Father, who art in heaven, | hallowed | be Thy | name; || Thy kingdom come, Thy will be done on | earth, : as it | is in | heaven;
2. Give us this | day our | daily | bread; || And forgive us our debts, as | we for- | give our | debtors.
3. And lead us not into temptation, but de- | liver | us from | evil; || For Thine is the kingdom, and the power, and the glory, for- | ever. | A- | men.

84. Earnestly Pray.

HARLEY ANDERSON. GEO. BEAVERSON.

Andante

1. In sym-pa-thy for those who weep, For tempt-ed ones who fall;
2. For homes made des-o-late by sin, For reck-less souls who stray;
3. For those who vain-ly sigh for rest, From whom all hopes have fled;
4. For men long va-liant for the truth In con-flict strong and brave,

For those who soon must si-lent sleep Beneath death's gloomy pall;
For err-ing ones whom love may win, In ten-der pit-y pray.
For those so long by fear oppressed, Now mourning for their dead;
Who no-bly strive our way-ward youth From sin and death to save;

CHORUS. *Faster.*

Earn-est-ly pray,............ trust-ful-ly pray,............
Earn-est-ly pray, trust-ful-ly pray,

The Lord............ will sure-ly hear;............
The Lord will sure-ly an-swer pray'r, will sure-ly an-swer pray'r;

Earn-est-ly pray,............ and trust His word,............
Earn-est-ly pray, trust to His word,

Copyright, 1894, by Geo. Beaverson.

Earnestly Pray. Concluded.

Amazing Grace.

NEWTON. J. G. FOOTE.

1. A-maz-ing grace! how sweet the sound, That sav'd a wretch like me,
2. 'Twas grace that taught my heart to fear, And grace my fears re-lieved;
3. Thro' ma-ny dan-gers, toils and snares I have al-read-y come;

I once was lost but now am found, Was blind but now I see.
How pre-cious did that grace ap-pear, The hour I first be-lieved.
'Tis grace has brought me safe thus far, And grace will lead me home.

D. S.—Was sav'd by grace, am kept by grace, This theme my song shall be.

CHORUS.

A-maz-ing grace! a-maz-ing grace, How sweet its sound to me,

From " New Hymns, by per."

Take My Hand, Dear Father.

"For I the Lord thy God will hold thy right hand."—Isa. xli: 13.

Mrs. E. C. Ellsworth. Alto Solo. Chas. Edw. Prior.

1. Take my hand, dear Father, Lead me safely through;
2. Take my hand, dear Father, Lest I meet a snare,
3. Take my hand, dear Father, Be my guard and guide.

For the gate is narrow, And the way is new.
And my feet should stumble While I'm unaware.
Nought shall ever harm me, While I'm near Thy side.

CHORUS.

Take my hand, oh, take it, Hold me close to Thee;
For with Thee in safety, Hold then, hold Thou me.

Copyright, 1894, by Chas. Edw. Prior.

Sometime the Veil will be Lifted. Concluded. 89

CHORUS.

Yes, sometime the veil will be lift-ed, The mists then will all clear a-way;
Within the bright sunshine of glo-ry All darkness will turn in-to day.

Song of Praise.

J. W. W. J. W. WARD.

1. Give thanks, all ye peo-ple, And praise ye the Lord; Re-joice in His mer-cy, Re-ly on His word. With joy-ous ho-san-nas And anthems proclaim His goodness and kindness, And worship His name, His name.
2. The wells of sal-va-tion Are flow-ing for thee; Oh! draw from the wa-ters So cleans-ing and free. The clear, crys-tal foun-tain, So sparkling and pure, Shall quench all thy longings, Refresh and en-dure, en-dure.
3. Oh! look un-to heav-en For guid-ance each day; Still cling to God's prom-ise, And la-bor and pray. For soon in His king-dom, The new song we'll sing, Where glad hal-le-lu-jahs, Resound to our King, our King.

Copyright, 1894, by W. S. Weeden.

Soldiers of the Lord. Concluded. 91

on,........ If we nev-er faint nor fal-ter, we shall
we're marching on,

sure-ly nev-er fail, For the Lord has promis'd that we shall prevail.

Nothing but Thy Blood.

Words arr. by J. W. VAN DE VENTER.   Music arr. by W. S. WEEDEN.

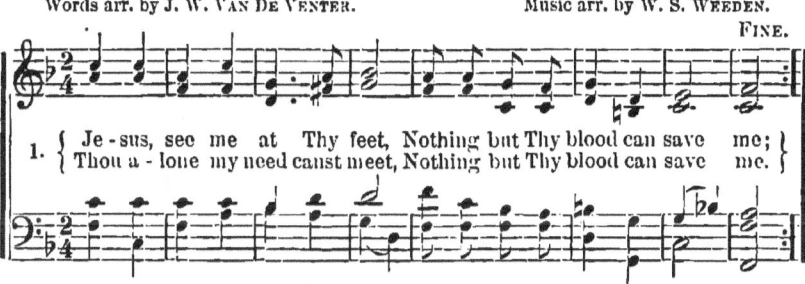

1. { Je-sus, see me at Thy feet, Nothing but Thy blood can save me;
     { Thou a-lone my need canst meet, Nothing but Thy blood can save me.

D.C.—To my cross, O Lamb of God, Nothing but Thy blood can save me.

REFRAIN.

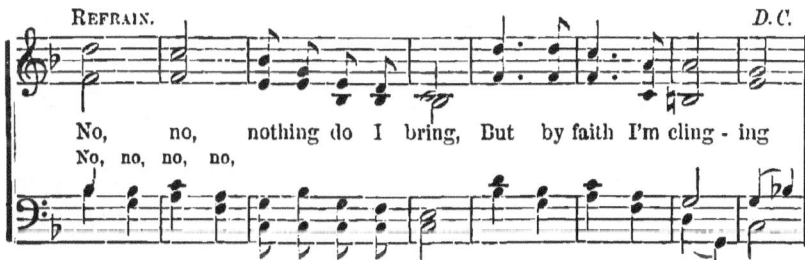

No, no, nothing do I bring, But by faith I'm cling-ing
No, no, no, no,

2 See my heart, Lord, torn with grief,
  Precious Savior, send relief.

3 As I am, oh, hear me pray,
  I can come no other way.

4 All that I can do is vain,
  I can ne'er remove a stain.

5 Lord, I cast myself on Thee,
  From my guilt, oh, set me free.

Copyright, 1894, by W. S. Weeden.

Consecration Hymn.

C. H. PAYNE, D.D., L.L.D.
W. S. WEEDEN.

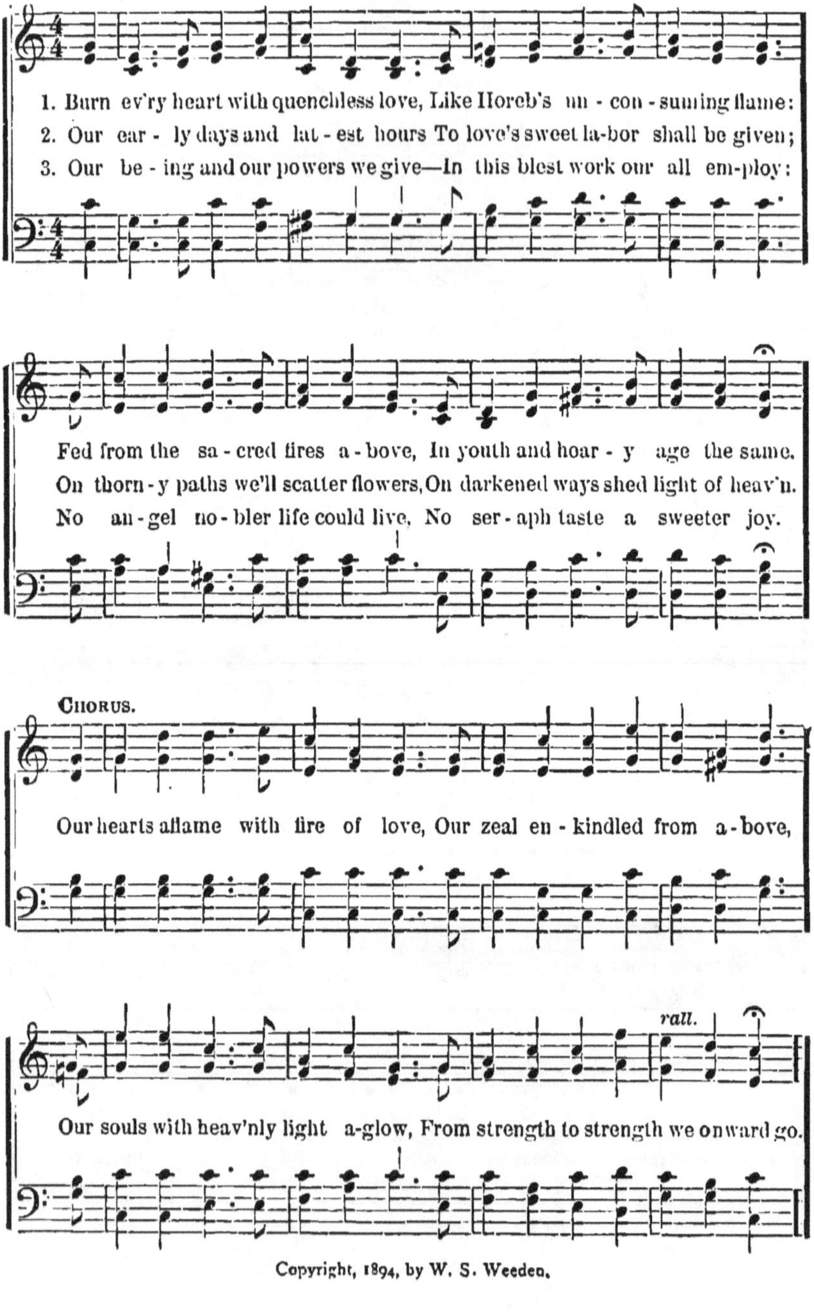

1. Burn ev'ry heart with quenchless love, Like Horeb's un - con - suming flame:
2. Our ear - ly days and lat - est hours To love's sweet la - bor shall be given;
3. Our be - ing and our powers we give—In this blest work our all em - ploy;

Fed from the sa - cred fires a - bove, In youth and hoar - y age the same.
On thorn - y paths we'll scatter flowers, On darkened ways shed light of heav'n.
No an - gel no - bler life could live, No ser - aph taste a sweeter joy.

Chorus.

Our hearts aflame with fire of love, Our zeal en - kindled from a - bove,

Our souls with heav'nly light a - glow, From strength to strength we onward go.

Copyright, 1894, by W. S. Weeden.

96. Onward Up the Highway.

Words and Music by J. W. Van De Venter.

1. Onward up the highway, To the promised land, Moves the gospel ar-my, Jesus in command; See the host advancing, On to victory! Marching up to Canaan, From captivity.
2. Onward up the highway, Vanquishing the foe, Following the Savior; Shouting as we go. Full and free salvation, Life for evermore; Marching to the homeland, On the other shore.
3. Onward up the highway, See the eastern sky, Radiant with sunshine—Morning draweth nigh. Soon the gates will open, Angel hosts appear; Onward, Christian soldier, Victory is near.

CHORUS.

When the struggle here is over, And the conquest is complete, We will lay aside our armor, Sweetly rest at Jesus' feet:

Copyright, 1894, by J. W. Van De Venter.

Onward Up the Highway. Concluded. 97

We will lay a-side our ar-mor, Sweetly rest at Je-sus' feet.

We Praise Thee, O Lord.

Rev. Wm. Appel.   A. Beirly.

1. We praise Thee, O Lord, For the smile of Thy face, For the health of Thy
2. We praise Thee, O Lord, For the light of Thy love, For the dew of Thy
3. We praise Thee, O Lord, For the strength of Thine arm, For Thy care and pro-
4. We praise Thee, O Lord, For Thy coming a-gain, For Thy glo-ri-ous

CHORUS.

sun-shine, The pow'r of Thy grace.
mer-cy That comes from a-bove.
-tec-tion That shields us from harm.
kingdom, Thy won-der-ful reign.

We praise Thee, dear Savior, A-gain and a-gain, We praise Thee, hal-le-lu-jah! for-ev-er a-men.

From "Golden Grain, No. 1," by per. of A. Beirly, publisher.

Go Preach the Gospel Tidings. Concluded.

He died that we might be redeemed; Oh, tell the wond'rous sto-ry.

Cling.

Anon.   GEO. BEAVERSON.

1. Cling to the Might-y One, Cling in thy grief, Cling to the Ho-ly One, He gives re-lief: Cling to the Gracious One, Cling in thy pain; Cling to the Faithful One, He will sus-tain.
2. Cling to the Liv-ing One, Cling in thy woe; Cling to the Liv-ing One, Through all be-low; Cling to the Pardoning One, He speaketh peace, Cling to the Healing One, Anguish shall cease.
3. Cling to the Bleed-ing One, Cling to His side, Cling to the Ris-en One, In Him a-bide; Cling to the Com-ing One, Hope shall a-rise, Cling to the Reigning One, Joy lights thine eyes.

Copyright, 1894, by Geo. Beaverson.

108. The Kingdom Shall Endure.

C. W. RAY.
GEO. BEAVERSON.

1. The Kingdom of the Lord............ For ev - er shall en-dure;............ The prom - ise of His word......... For-ev - er shall be sure. He will...... His ho - ly cause maintain, He will....... ex-tend His
2. The Islands of the sea............Shall sweet - est off'rings bring;......... And songs......... of ju - bi-lee............ They grate - ful - ly shall sing. The world....... shall bend with trembling awe, And haste..... to ex - e-

1. The Kingdom of the Lord, The Kingdom of the Lord For-ev-er shall endure, For-ev-er shall endure; The prom-ise of His word, The promise of His word, For-ev-er shall be sure, For-ev-er shall be sure. He will His ho-ly cause maintain, He will ex-tend His
2. The Isl-ands of the sea Shall sweet of-ferings bring, Shall sweet of-fer-ings bring, Shall sweet of-ferings bring; And songs, ju-bi-lee songs, Shall they gratefully sing, Shall they gratefully sing, Shall they gratefully sing. The world shall bend with trem-bling awe, And haste to ex - e-

Copyright, 1894, by C. W. Ray.

The Kingdom Shall Endure. Concluded. 109

righteous reign, His conquests reach from shore to shore, Till heathen tribes His
-cute His law; While small and great before Him fall, And crown their Maker
righteous reign, His conquests reach from shore to shore, Till heathen tribes His
-cute His law; While small and great be - fore Him fall, And crown their Mak-er

CHORUS.

name a - dore. The King - - dom of the Lord............ For
Lord of all. The Isl - - ands of the sea............ Shall
name a - dore. The kingdom of the Lord, The king-dom of the Lord For-
Lord of all. The is-lands of the sea, The is-lands of the sea Shall

ev - - - er shall en - dure, The prom - - ise of His
sweet - - - est off'rings bring, And songs...... .. of ju-bi-
ev - er shall endure, For - ev - er shall endure, The promise of His word, The
sweet offerings bring, Shall sweet offerings bring, And songs, jubilee songs, They

word .. .. For - ev - - - er shall be sure!
- lee .... They grate - - - ful-ly shall sing.
prom-ise of His word, For - ev - er shall be sure, For - ev - er shall be sure!
shall grateful-ly sing, And songs, ju - bi-lee songs They shall grateful-ly sing.

5 Do you remember the letter that came,
 Telling how that dear mother had died?
And while dying, she prayed God to lead her boy home
 To his heav'n, and a place by her side?

6 Will you give heed to these mem'ries to-day,
 And turn to the Savior, your friend?
Believe Him, and trust Him, and serve Him alway,
 He'll forgive you, and save to the end.

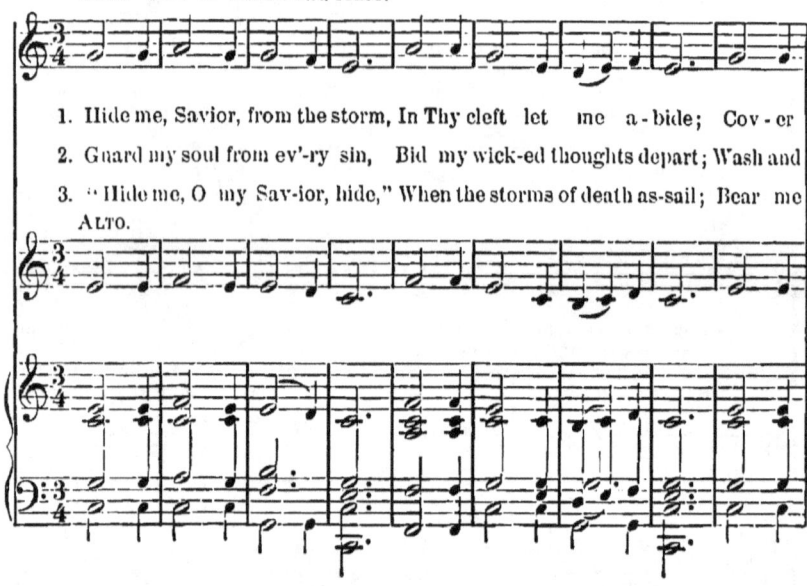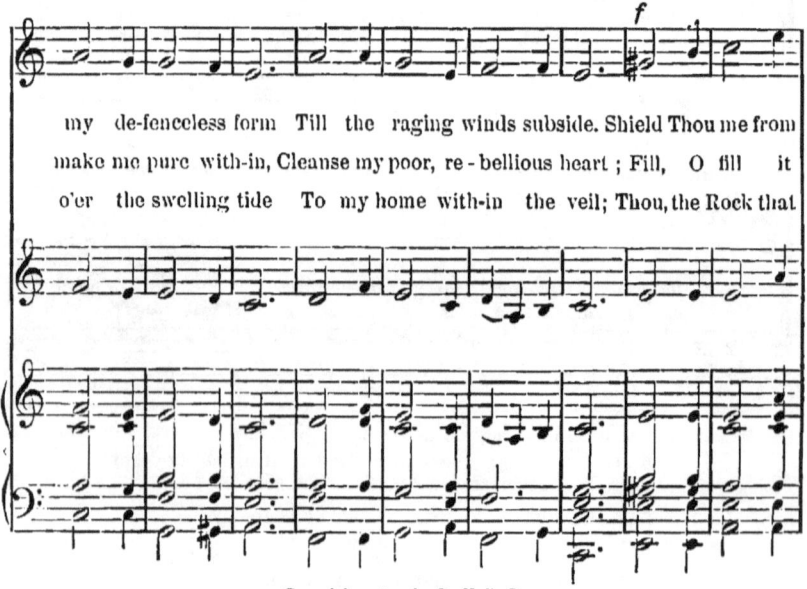

Hide Me. Concluded. 113

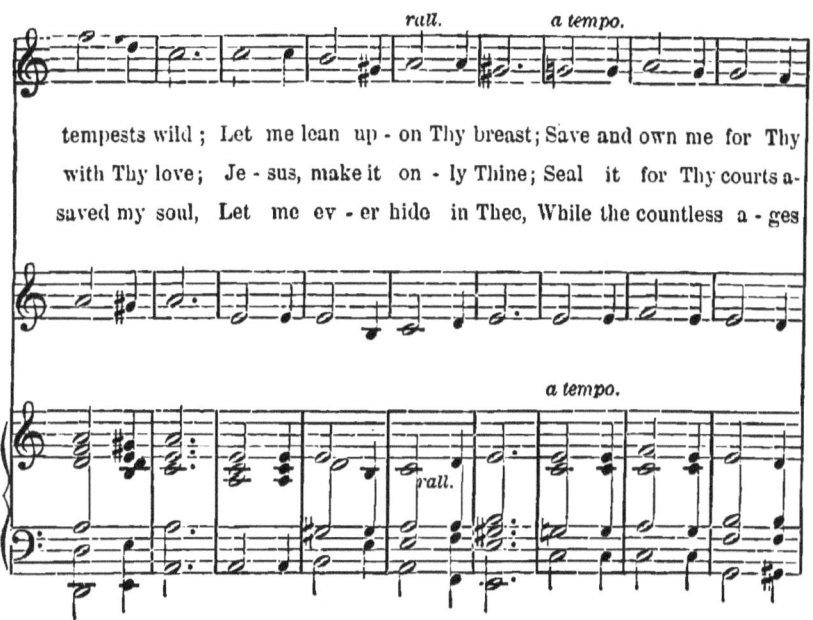

tempests wild; Let me lean up-on Thy breast; Save and own me for Thy
with Thy love; Je - sus, make it on - ly Thine; Seal it for Thy courts a-
saved my soul, Let me ev - er hide in Thee, While the countless a - ges

child; On Thy bo-som let me rest, On Thy bo-som let me rest.
- bove With Thy pre-cious love di-vine, With Thy pre-cious love di-vine.
roll On through all e - ter - ni - ty, On through all e - ter - ni - ty.

The Cross of Jesus Lifts Me. 117

A heathen ruler who had heard the story of the cross was dying. He said to his attendants, "Make me a cross and lay me upon it." They did so, and as he lay there dying, he laid hold of the blood of Christ and said, "It lifts me up, it lifts me, it lifts me, it lifts me."

J. W. Van De Venter.   W. S. Weeden.

1. O, the cross of Je-sus lifts me, Lifts me up and makes me free;
2. O, the cross of Je-sus lifts me, Lifts me in-to per-fect rest;
3. O, the cross of Je-sus lifts me, Lifts me up to fall no more;

On a sol-id sure foun-da-tion, On the rock He cleft for me.
Where the surg-ing bil-lows nev-er Roll a-cross my peace-ful breast.
Up-ward, up-ward, ev-er ris-ing, Till it touch-es yon-der shore.

Though tempta-tions may as-sail me, Thro' the pre-cious blood I rise;
High-er, high-er still it lifts me Thro' the vast ex-panse of blue,
Ra-diant with im-mor-tal glo-ry Je-sus crowns me His a-bove,

I can feel the lift-ing pow-er Of the bless-ed sac-ri-fice.
Up-ward till the hills of glo-ry Roll their grandeur in-to view.
Saved to live and bask for-ev-er In the sun-shine of His love.

Copyright, 1894, by W. S. Weeden.

118. We'll Never Say Good-bye.

J. G. D.
J. G. DAILEY.

1. Yes, the sor-row, pain and woe, That we find where'er we go,
2. Ties of friendship, strong and true, Bind your dear-est friend to you;
3. Fa-ther, moth-er, children dear, Whom we've lov'd and cherish'd here,
4. Praise the Lord, the time will come When we'll all be gathered home,

Fill with bit-ter tears the weeping eyes, When we reach the parting strand,
And the hours unheed-ed, swift-ly fly, But the time will come to thee
Wait our com-ing in the by and by; What a meet-ing that will be,
There to live and reign with God on high; End-less prais-es we shall sing,

And we clasp the parting hand, And we sad-ly speak the last good-bye.
When those ties will severed be, And you'll sad-ly speak the last good-bye.
When each oth-er's face we see, And we'll nev-er, nev-er say good-bye.
In the presence of the King, And we'll nev-er, nev-er say good-bye.

CHORUS.

1-2. But we'll never say good-bye, o-ver yonder, We will never say good-
3-4. We will, etc.

bye, o-ver yon-der, As we walk the gold-en street, And each

Used by per. of J. G. Dailey, owner of copyright.

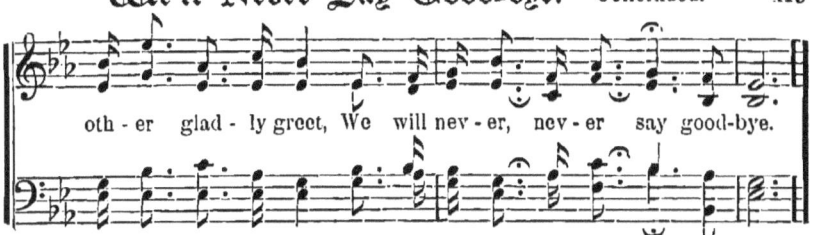

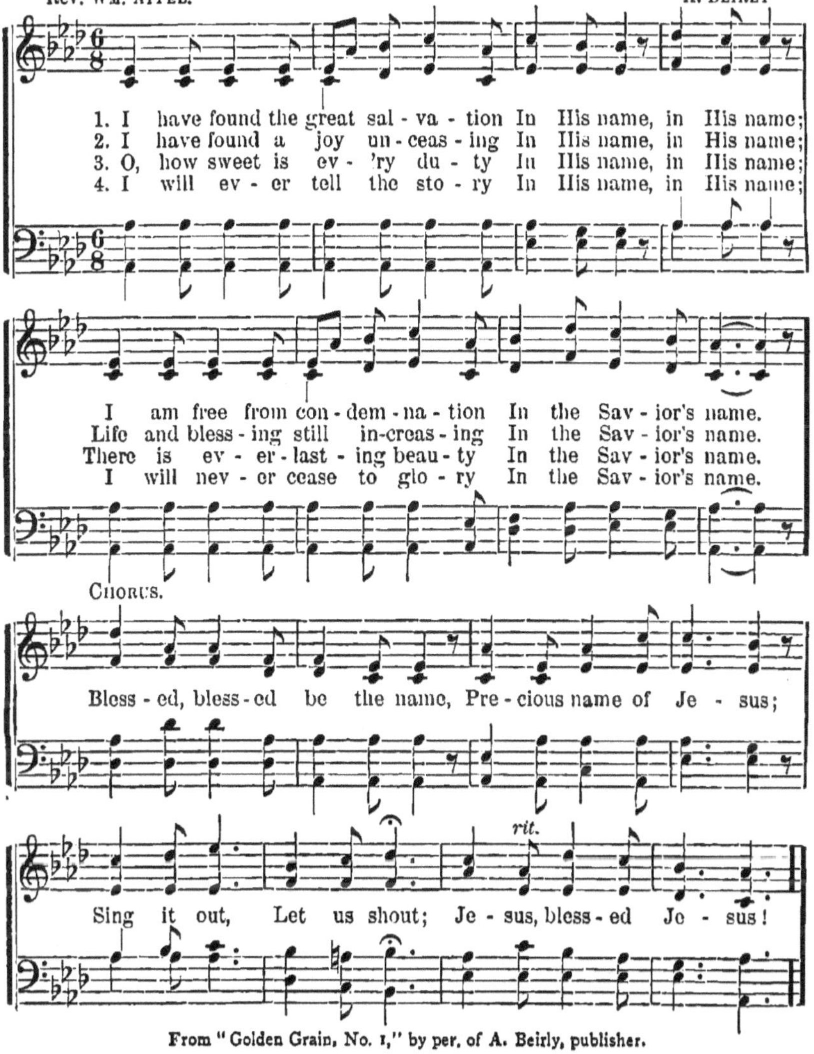

I'm Going to Jesus To-night. 125

A little boy was taken fatally ill, and when he was told that he could not live, he said to his mother, "It is dark; I'm afraid to die." Then he closed his eyes a few moments in prayer. Arousing suddenly, as he seemed to catch a glimpse of the better world, he said, "Mother, don't weep for your boy; it is all right now; an angel has shown me the way; I'm going to Jesus to-night."

Words and Music by J. W. VAN DE VENTER.

1. O moth-er, don't weep for your boy, A beau-ti-ful land is in sight;
An an-gel has shown me the way, I'm go-ing to Je-sus to-night.

2. The pathway was once ve-ry dark, But God sent a beau-ti-ful light,
And heav-en is now ve-ry near, I'm go-ing to Je-sus to-night.

3. Tho' I was so reckless and wild, The Sav-ior has made it all right;
I'm will-ing and read-y to die, I'm go-ing to Je-sus to-night.

CHORUS.

I'm go-ing to Je-sus to-night, I'm go-ing to Je-sus to-night;
An an-gel has shown me the way, I'm go-ing to Je-sus to-night.

Copyright, 1894, by J. W. Van De Venter.

Song of Peace. Concluded.

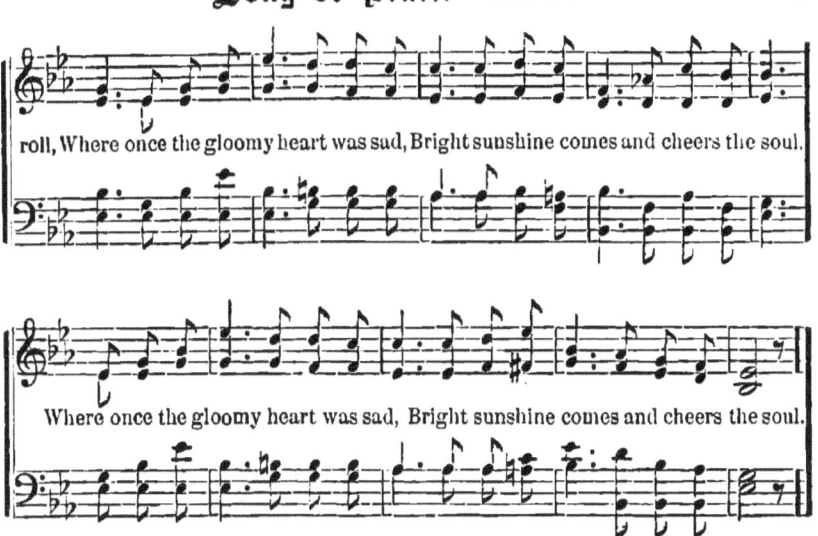

roll, Where once the gloomy heart was sad, Bright sunshine comes and cheers the soul.

Where once the gloomy heart was sad, Bright sunshine comes and cheers the soul.

Come, Brother, Come!

J. W. W. J. W. WARD.

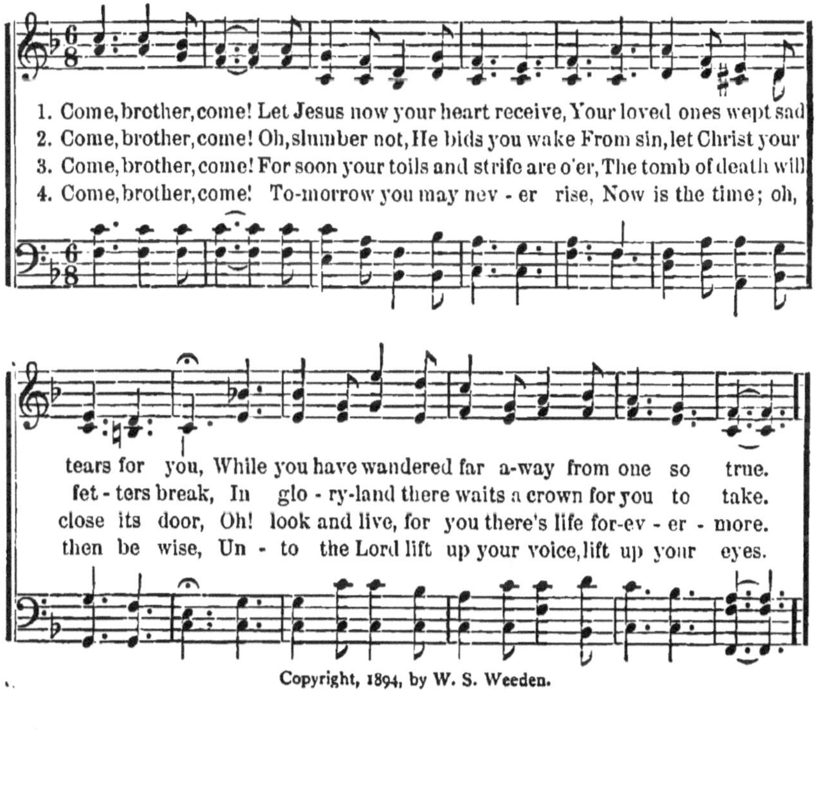

1. Come, brother, come! Let Jesus now your heart receive, Your loved ones wept sad
2. Come, brother, come! Oh, slumber not, He bids you wake From sin, let Christ your
3. Come, brother, come! For soon your toils and strife are o'er, The tomb of death will
4. Come, brother, come! To-morrow you may nev - er rise, Now is the time; oh,

tears for you, While you have wandered far a-way from one so true.
fet - ters break, In glo - ry-land there waits a crown for you to take.
close its door, Oh! look and live, for you there's life for-ev - er - more.
then be wise, Un - to the Lord lift up your voice, lift up your eyes.

Copyright, 1894, by W. S. Weeden.

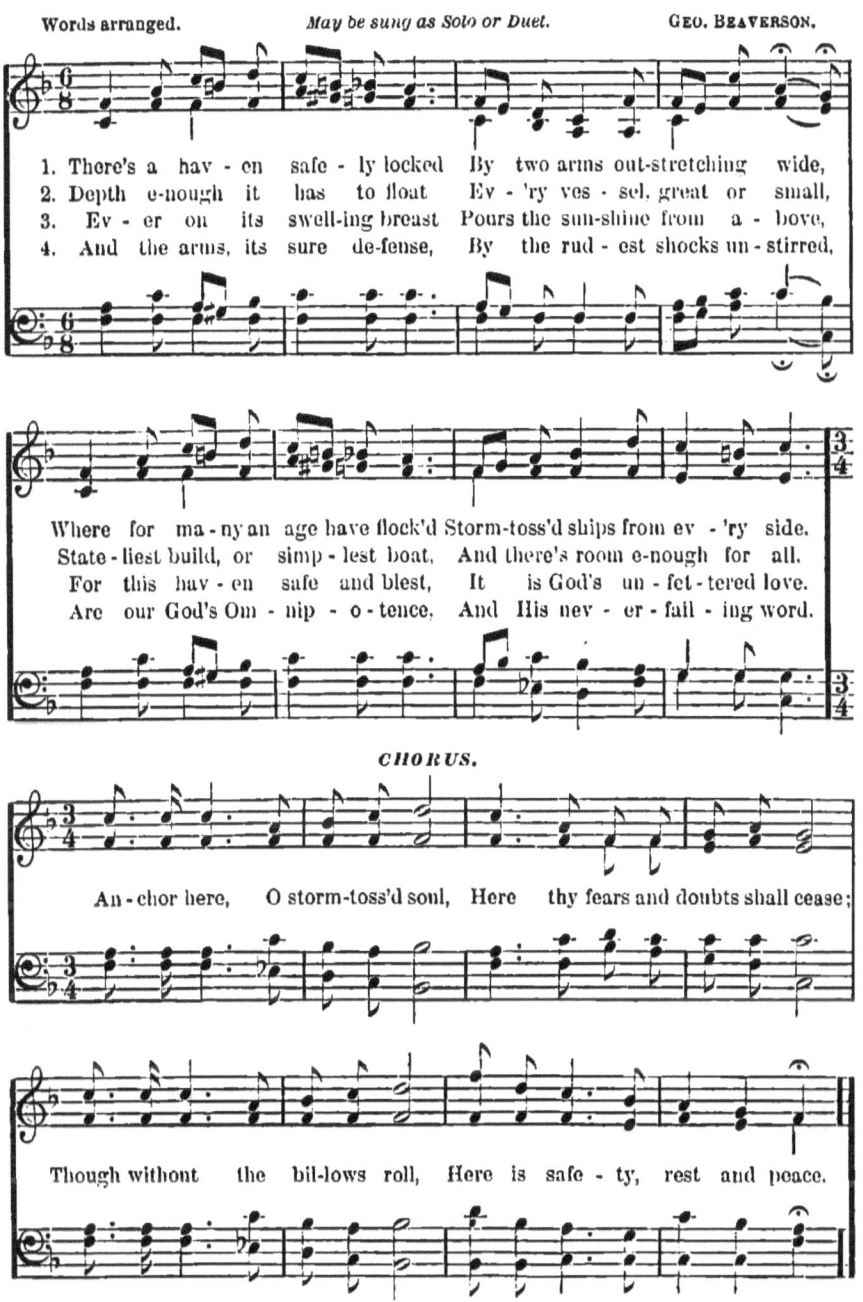

Send the Light. Concluded. 131

Elmhurst. L. M.

GEO. F. ROSCHE.

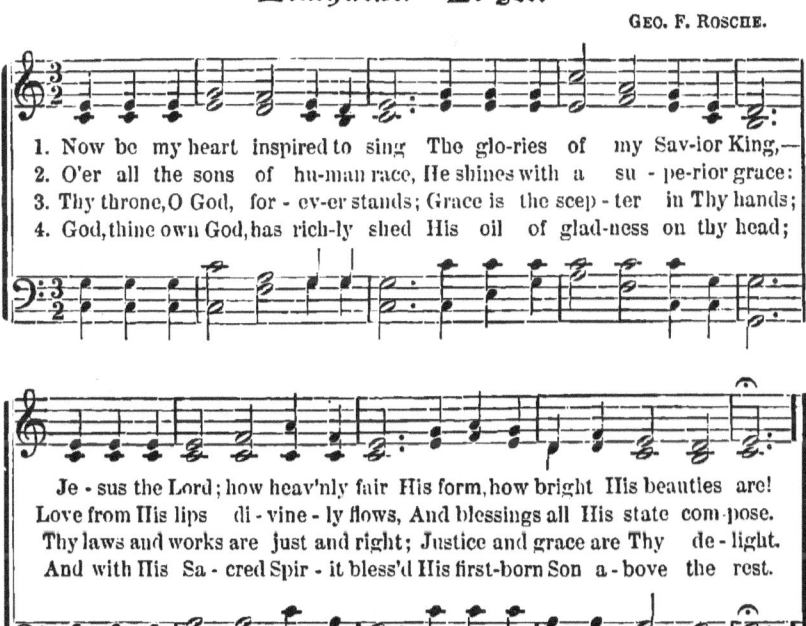

1. Now be my heart inspired to sing The glo-ries of my Sav-ior King,— Je-sus the Lord; how heav'nly fair His form, how bright His beauties are!
2. O'er all the sons of hu-man race, He shines with a su-pe-rior grace: Love from His lips di-vine-ly flows, And blessings all His state com-pose.
3. Thy throne, O God, for-ev-er stands; Grace is the scep-ter in Thy hands; Thy laws and works are just and right; Justice and grace are Thy de-light.
4. God, thine own God, has rich-ly shed His oil of glad-ness on thy head; And with His Sa-cred Spir-it bless'd His first-born Son a-bove the rest.

Used by per. of Geo. F. Rosche, owner of copyright.

The Wanderer's Return. Concluded. 137

But now do-cile to Thy lead - ing I shall be.
Lo! I come, repentant, guide me, Gen - tle Lord.
Me, Thy precious blood all-sav - ing, Cleansed for - e'er.
Not in darkness feeb-ly grop - ing— I AM FREE.

Gently Evening Bendeth.

Anon.
Dolce.
C. H. Rink. Arr. by G. B.

1. Gent - ly eve - ning bend - eth O - ver vale and hill;
2. Save the wood-brook's gush - ing, All things si - lent rest;
3. And no eve - ning bring - eth To its life re - lease;
4. Rest - less thus life flow - eth, Striv - eth in my breast;

Soft - ly peace de - scend - eth, And the world is still.
Hear its rest - less rush - ing, On t'ward o - cean's breast.
And no sweet bell ring - eth, O'er its wave - lets, peace.
God a - lone be - stow - eth Tran - quil eve - ning rest.

Copyright, 1894, by Geo. Beaverson.

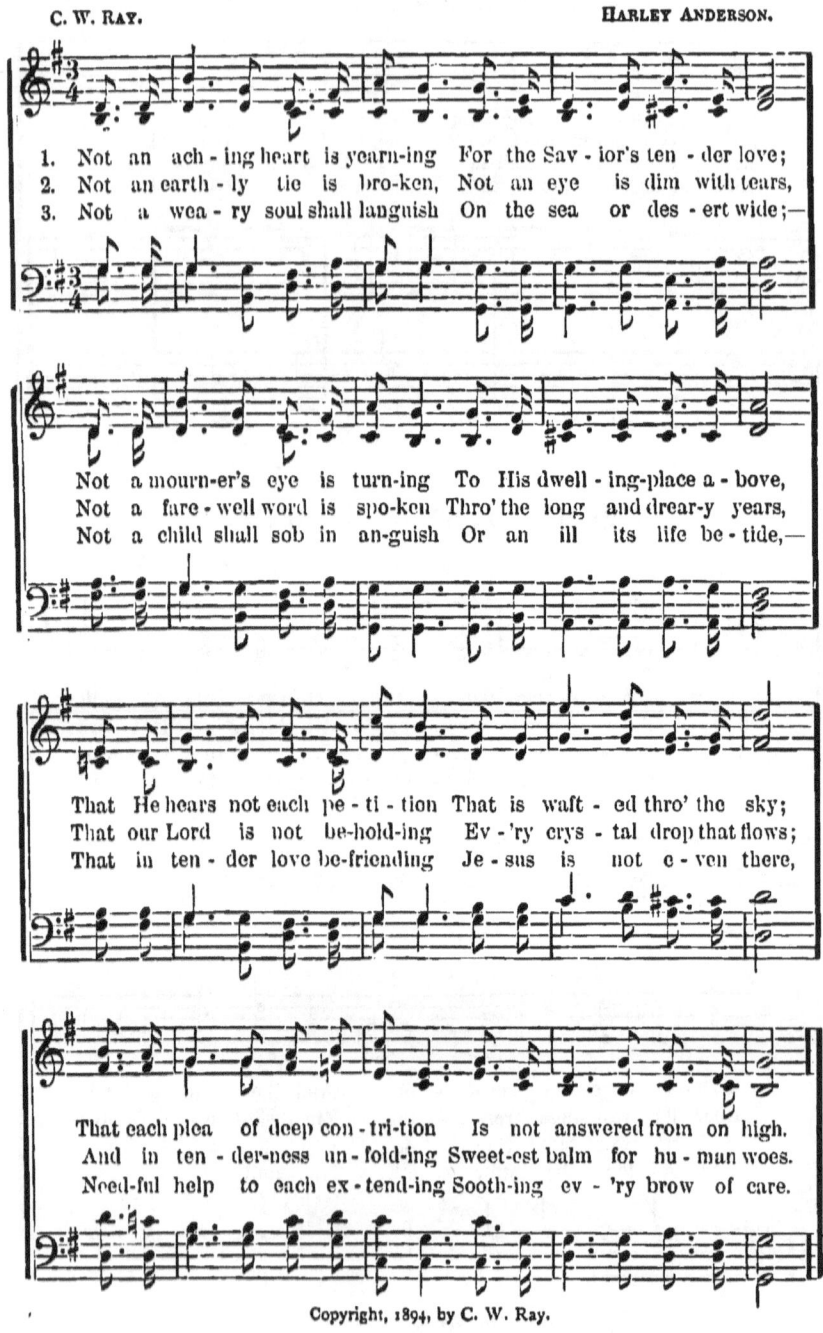

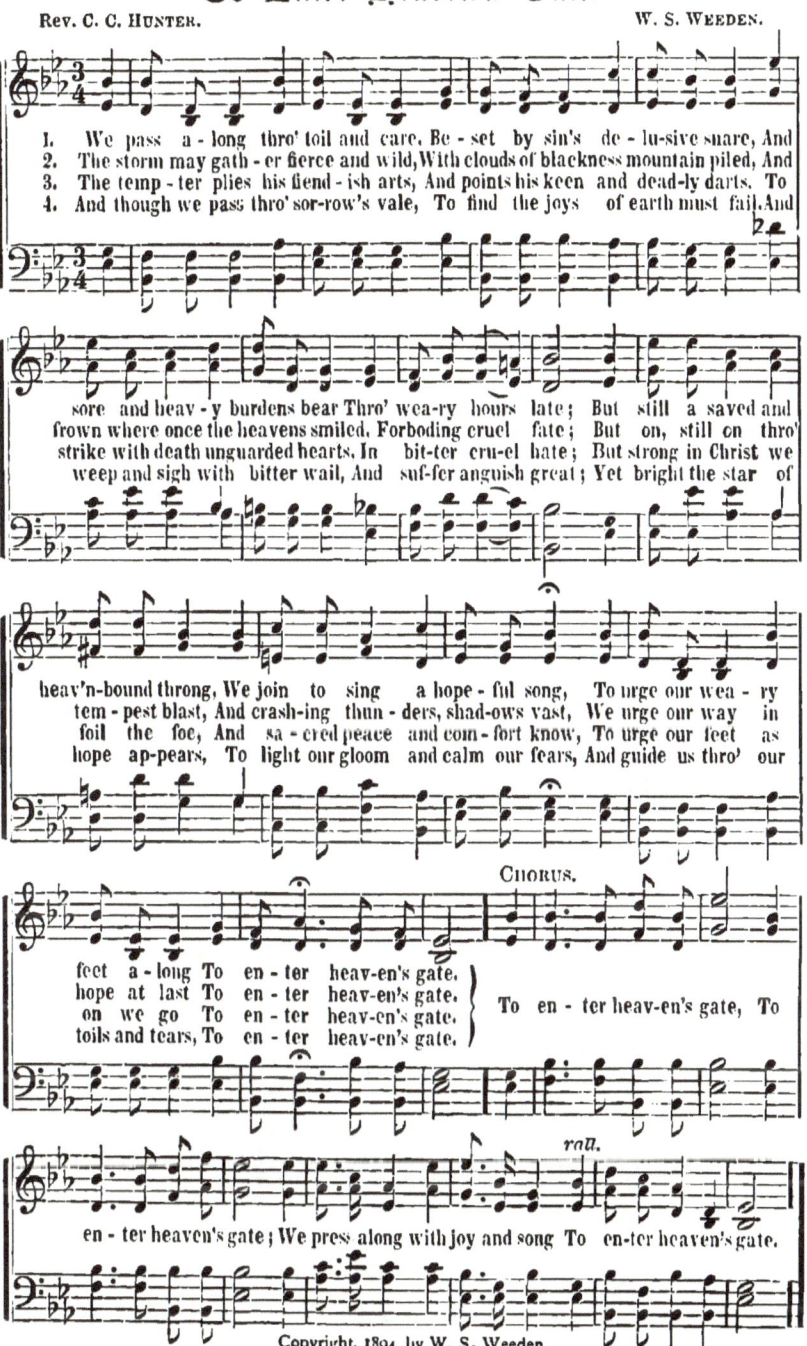

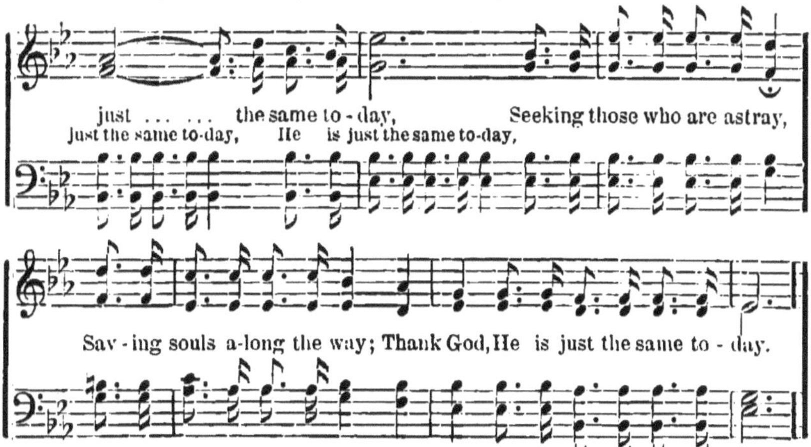

Just the Same To-day. Concluded. 141

just .... the same to-day, Seeking those who are astray,
Just the same to-day, He is just the same to-day,

Sav-ing souls a-long the way; Thank God, He is just the same to-day.

Time's Restless Tide.

LAURA E. NEWELL.   MALE QUARTET.   J. W. WARD.

1. Adown life's vale we wander, Borne swift-ly on for-ev-er, For
2. The friends we love and cherish, With sweetest blos-soms per-ish, And
3. Adown life's vale we wander, We near the si-lent riv-er, With

time no hand can stay, None may recall to-day; We're borne adown time's
as they calm-ly sleep. A vig-il sad we keep, While borne adown time's
loved ones we'll abide, When past time's restless tide, We'll soon be past time's

rest-less tide, A - down time's restless tide, time's restless tide.
rest less tide, A - down time's restless tide, time's restless tide.
rest-less tide, Be - yond time's restless tide, time's restless tide.

Copyright, 1894, by W. S. Weeden.

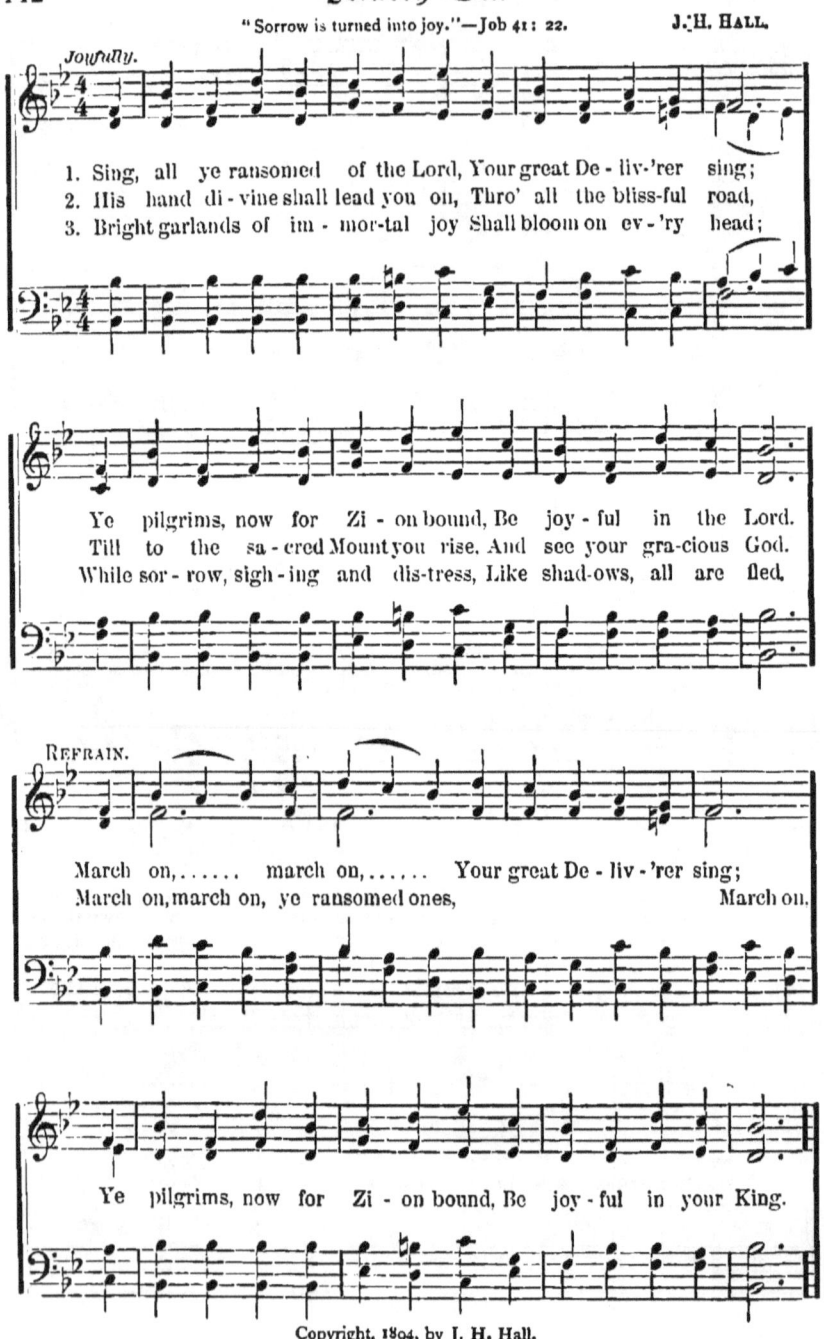

I Need Thee, Lord. 145

"Without me ye can do nothing."—John xv. 5.

Rev. E. A. Hoffman.   Chas. Edw. Prior. By per.

1. When cherish'd joys have taken wing, And sorrow wounds me with its sting,
2. When sin has robb'd me of my peace, And bro't me in - to sore dis-tress,
3. When at the cross in anguish bent, An humble, weeping pen - i - tent,
4. When strong temptations come to me To tear my trembling soul from Thee,

Then to Thy cross   I fond - ly cling, For then   I need Thee, Lord.
And left me 'reft   of hap - pi - ness, Oh, then   I need Thee, Lord.
My tears and all   my ef - forts spent, Oh, then   I need Thee, Lord.
Then to Thy cross   for help I flee, For then   I need Thee, Lord.

Chorus.

I need Thee, pre-cious Lord! In Thee my soul would hide!
In ev - 'ry time of need, Dear Christ, with me a - bide.

5. When longs my soul for deeper rest,
   To be with all Thy fullness blest,
   I lean me, then, upon Thy breast,
   For then I need Thee, Lord.

6. I need Thee, precious Lord, just **now**,
   As at the mercy-seat I bow,
   And offer up my solemn vow,
   Just now I need Thee, Lord.

Soldiers of the King. Concluded.

Good News Gone to Canaan.
JUBILEE SONG.

Arr. by W. S Weeden.

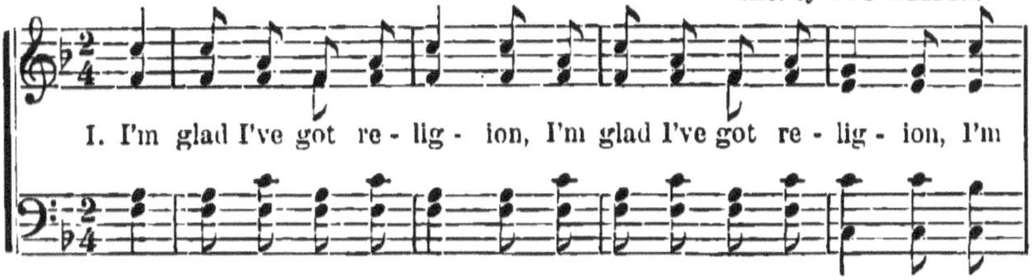

1. I'm glad I've got re-lig-ion, I'm glad I've got re-lig-ion, I'm glad I've got re-lig-ion, I'm on my way. Good news gone to Ca-na-an, Good news gone to Ca-na-an, Good news gone to Ca-na-an, I'm on my way.

2 I'll tell you how I got it,
 I'm on my way.

3 I gave my heart to Jesus,
 I'm on my way.

4 I'll tell you how I keep it,
 I'm on my way.

5 By watching and by praying,
 I'm on my way.

6 My all is on the altar,
 I'm on my way.

7 I'm believing and receiving,
 I'm on my way.

Copyright, 1894, by W. S. Weeden.

148 The Dying Boatman.

Dedicated to my Esteemed Friend W. S. Weeden.

Words and Music by J. W. Van De Venter.

Copyright, 1894, by J. W. Van De Venter.

The Dying Boatman. Concluded. 149

All the Way to Calvary. 151

Mrs. W. G. Moyer & I. H. M. I. H. Meredith. Cho. arr.

1. Oh, how dark the night that wrapt my spir-it round! Oh, how deep the woe my
2. Tremblingly a sin-ner bowed be-fore his face, Naught I knew of par-don,—
3. Oh, 'twas wondrous love the Sav-ior show'd for me, When He left His throne for

Sav-ior found When He walked a-cross the wa-ters of my soul,
God's free grace, Heard a voice so melt-ing, "Cease thy wild re-gret,
Cal-va-ry, When He trod the wine-press, trod it all a-lone,

CHORUS.

Bade my night dis-perse and made me whole.
Je-sus bought thy par-don, paid thy debt." } All the way to
Praise His name for-ev-er, make it known.

Cal-va-ry He went for me, He went for me, He went for me,

All the way to Cal-va-ry He went for me, He died to set me free.

Copyright, 1894, by I. H. Meredith.

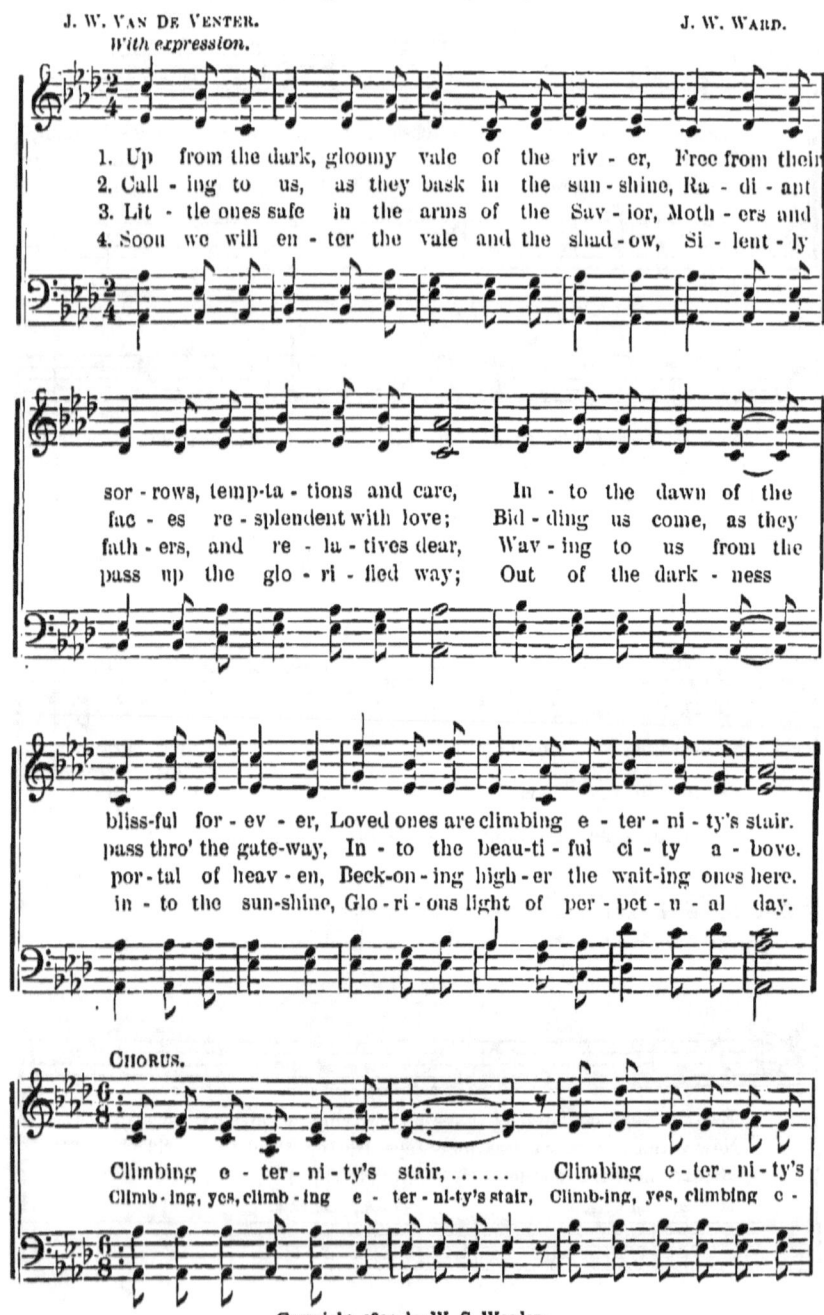

Climbing Eternity's Stair. Concluded. 157

Come to the Savior, Come.

CHAS. WESLEY.
Arr. by W. S. WEEDEN.

1. { Come, sinners, to the gos-pel feast; Come to the Sav-ior, come, }
   { Let ev-'ry soul be Je-sus' guest; Come to the Sav-ior, come. }
2. { Ye need not one be left be-hind; Come to the Sav-ior, come, }
   { For God hath bid-den all man-kind: Come to the Sav-ior, come. }

D.C.—For you He shed His pre-cious blood, Come to the Sav-ior, come.

REFRAIN.

Come to the Sav-ior, come,...... Come to the Sav-ior, come;

3 Sent by my Lord, on you I call;
  The invitation is to all.

4 Come all the world! come, sinner, thou
  All things in Christ are ready now.

5 Come, all ye souls by sin oppressed,
  Ye restless wand'rers after rest.

6 Ye poor, and maimed, and halt, and blind
  In Christ a hearty welcome find.

7 My message as from God receive;
  Ye all may come to Christ and live.

8 O let His love your hearts constrain,
  Nor suffer Him to die in vain.

Copyright, 1894, by W. S. Weeden.

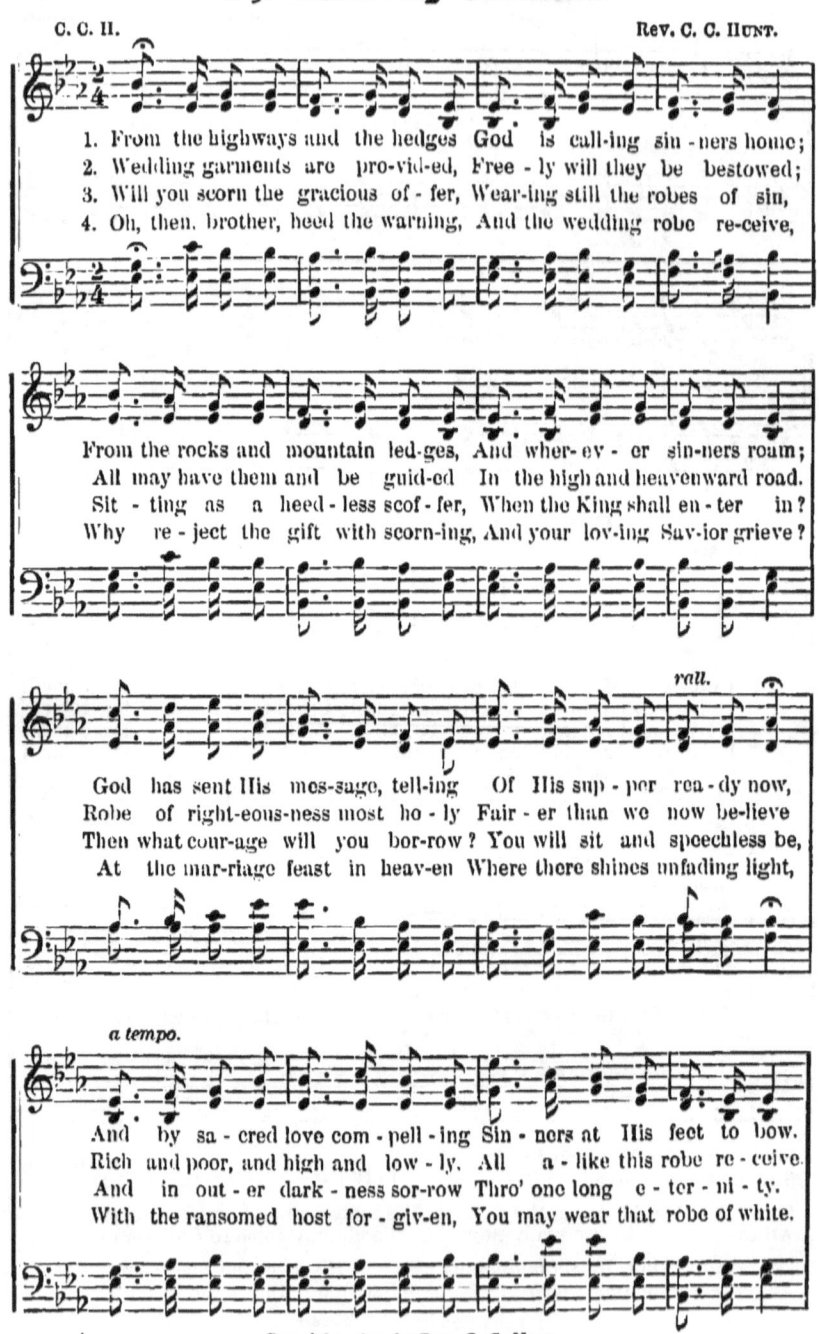

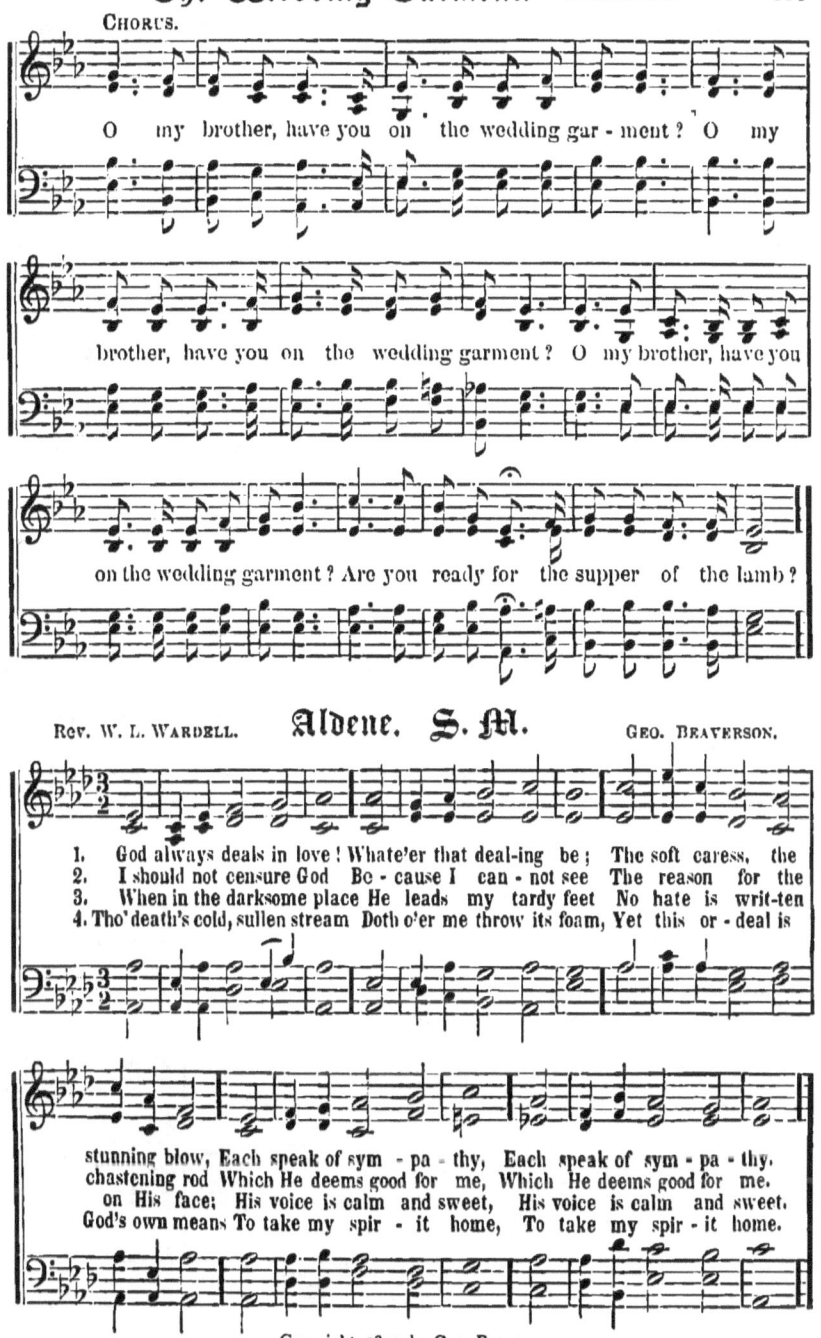

Hold Up the Light. Concluded.

161

Man-y a wan-der-er Out in the night, Peer-ing thro' darkness, No help with-in sight. Is your boy among them? Oh, hold up the light.

My Country, 'tis of Thee.

S. F. SMITH.
Tune, "America."

1 My country, 'tis of thee,
   Sweet land of liberty,
     Of thee I sing;
   Land where my fathers died,
   Land of the pilgrims' pride,
   From ev'ry mountain side
     Let freedom ring.

2 My native country, thee,
   Land of the noble free,
     Thy name I love;
   I love thy rocks and rills,
   Thy woods and templed hills;
   My heart with rapture thrills,
     Like that above.

3 Let music swell the breeze,
   And ring from all the trees
     Sweet freedom's song;
   Let mortal tongues awake,
   Let all that breathe partake,
   Let rocks their silence break,
     The sound prolong.

4 Our father's God, to Thee,
   Author of liberty,
     To Thee we sing;
   Long may our land be bright
   With freedom's holy light;
   Protect us by thy might,
     Great God, our King.

Our Country's Voice. Concluded. 163

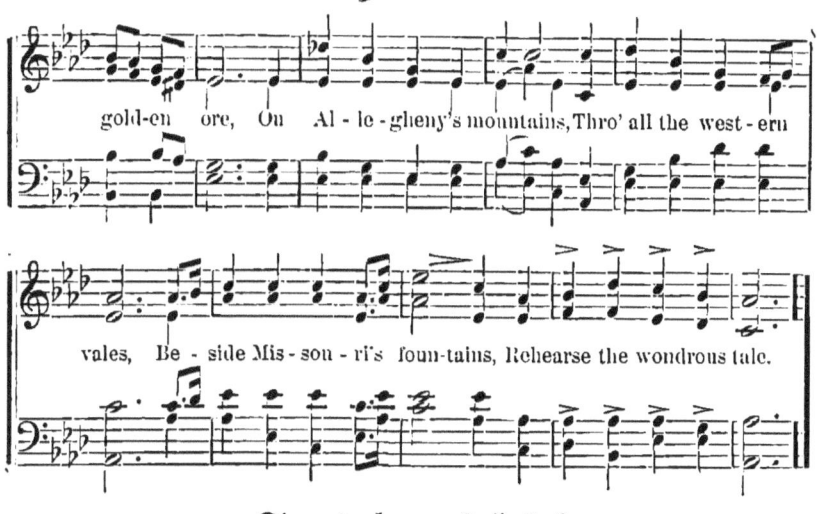

gold-en ore, On Al-le-gheny's mountains, Thro' all the west-ern vales, Be-side Mis-sou-ri's foun-tains, Rehearse the wondrous tale.

Gwendolen. 8, 5, 8, 3.
T. J. Davies, Mus. Bac.

1. Art thou wea-ry, art thou lan-guid, Art thou sore distressed?
2. Hath He marks to lead me to Him, If He be my guide?
3. Is there di-a-dem, as mon-arch, That His brow a-dorns?

"Come to me," saith One, "and com-ing, Be at rest."
"In His feet, and hands, are wound-prints, And His side."
"Yea, a crown in ve-ry sure-ty, But of thorns."

4 If I find Him, if I follow,
   What His guerdon here?
"Many a sorrow, many a labor,
   Many a tear."

5 If I still hold closely to Him,
   What hath He at last?
"Sorrow vanquished, labor ended,
   Jordan past!"

6 If I ask Him to receive me,
   Will He say me nay?
"Not till earth and not till heaven
   Pass away!"

7 Finding, following, keeping, struggling,
   Is He sure to bless?
Angels, martyrs, prophets, virgins,
   Answer "Yes!"

Copyright, 1894, by T. J. Davies.

A Little While with Jesus. Concluded.

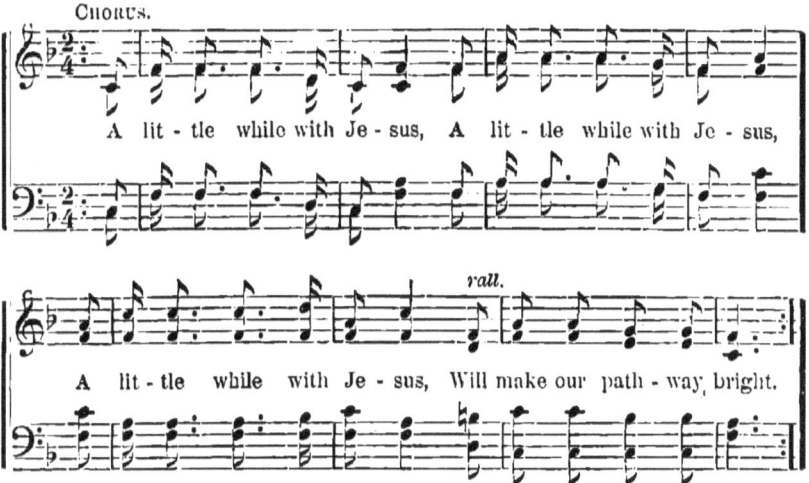

I Can, I Will, I Do Believe.

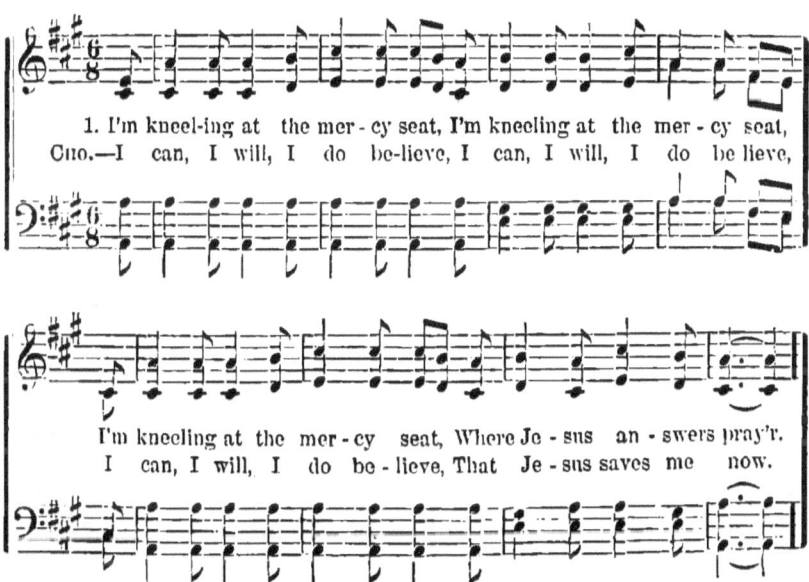

2 Refining fire, go through my heart,
   Refining fire, go through my heart,
   Refining fire, go through my heart,
     Illuminate my soul.

3 O, that it now from heaven might fall,
   O, that it now from heaven might fall,
   O, that it now from heaven might fall,
     And all my sins consume.

If We Would but See the Way. Concluded. 167

D. S. ℈.

Bear a light......... where'er we go;
Bear a light where'er we go, Bear a light where'er we go.

Day by Day.

EVA T. POOLE.   Tune, WARDELL.   G. B SOTTIS.

1. Trust in the Lord to hide thee, Wait on the Lord to guide thee; So shall no ill be-tide thee,
2. Rise with His fear be-fore thee, Tell of the love He bore thee; Sleep with His shad-ow o'er thee,
3. Clouds with their sil-ver lin-ing, Hopes and fears in-ter-twin-ing, God Him-self thro' them shin-ing,
4. Such may be thy sur-round-ing, Still let His praise be sound-ing, Praise for His grace a-bound-ing,

Day by day; So shall no ill be-tide thee, Day by day.
Day by day; Sleep with His shad-ow o'er thee, Day by day.
Day by day; God Him-self thro' them shining, Day by day.
Day by day; Praise for His grace a-bound-ing, Day by day.

Copyright, 1894, by Geo. Beaverson.

Fighting Underneath the Cross. Concluded. 169

CHORUS. *Marcato.*

Fight - ing un - der-neath the cross, We shall nev - er suf - fer loss;

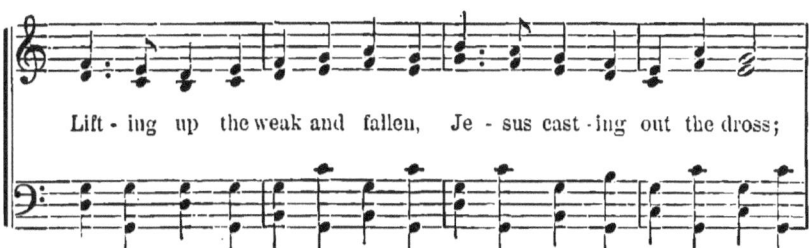

Lift - ing up the weak and fallen, Je - sus cast - ing out the dross;

Mak - ing our sal - va - tion free, Through the blood of Cal - va - ry;

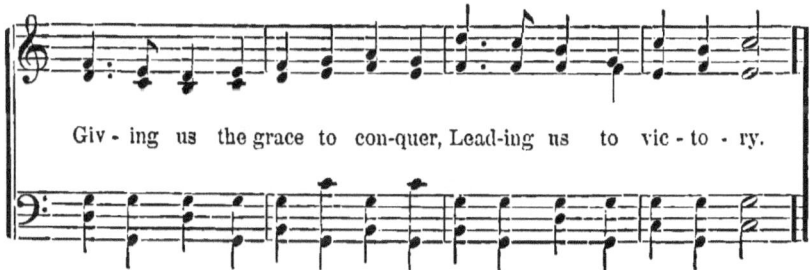

Giv - ing us the grace to con-quer, Lead-ing us to vic - to - ry.

Let it Shine. Concluded. 171

Hold up the light, For thousands are wait-ing to see, Let it shine where the night is the dark-est, To show where the dangers may be.

Weeden. C. M.

Rev. W. L. WARDELL.   GEO. BEAVERSON.

1. I love to med-i-tate, O God! Up-on Thy ho-ly word;
2. How sweet it is to think up-on Thy mer-cy and Thy grace:
3. Like Jes-se's son of old-en time, We of-fer praise to Thee;

I love to lean up-on Thy rod, I love to lean up-on Thy rod,
As in this house of pray'r we come, As in this house of pray'r we come,
Oh, bless us now while at Thy shrine, Oh, bless us now while at Thy shrine,

I love to lean up-on Thy rod, A-mid the dis-mal flood.
As in this house of pray'r we come To seek Thy lov-ing face.
Oh, bless us now while at Thy shrine We hum-bly bend our knee.

Copyright, 1894, by Geo. Beaverson.

Glory to the Bleeding Lamb. 173

CARRIE ELLA BRECK.   GRANT C. TULLAR.

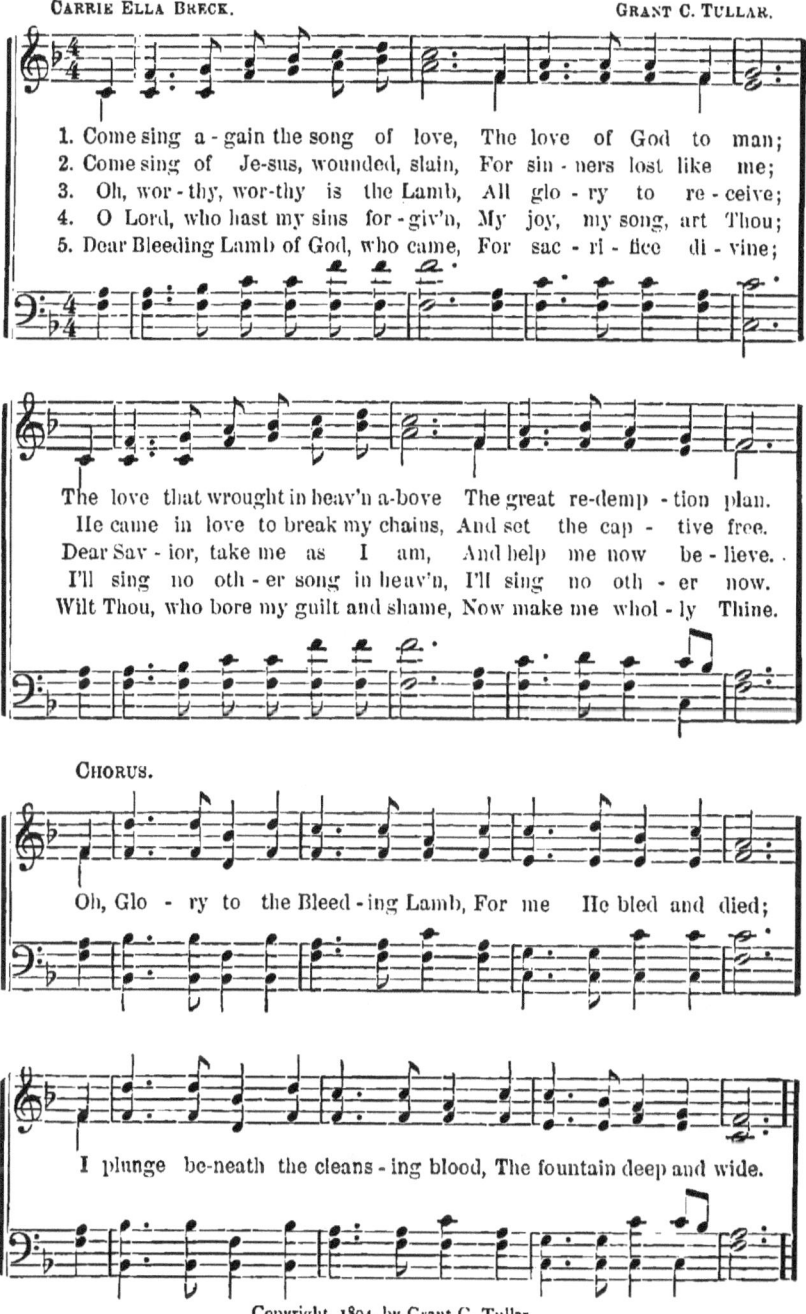

1. Come sing a-gain the song of love, The love of God to man;
2. Come sing of Je-sus, wounded, slain, For sin-ners lost like me;
3. Oh, wor-thy, wor-thy is the Lamb, All glo-ry to re-ceive;
4. O Lord, who hast my sins for-giv'n, My joy, my song, art Thou;
5. Dear Bleeding Lamb of God, who came, For sac-ri-fice di-vine;

The love that wrought in heav'n a-bove The great re-demp-tion plan.
He came in love to break my chains, And set the cap-tive free.
Dear Sav-ior, take me as I am, And help me now be-lieve.
I'll sing no oth-er song in heav'n, I'll sing no oth-er now.
Wilt Thou, who bore my guilt and shame, Now make me whol-ly Thine.

CHORUS.

Oh, Glo-ry to the Bleed-ing Lamb, For me He bled and died;

I plunge be-neath the cleans-ing blood, The fountain deep and wide.

Copyright. 1894, by Grant C. Tullar.

174. Wait! Wait! Jesus Will Come!

"And to wait for his Son from heaven."—Thess. 1:10.

E. S. U.   Rev. E. S. UFFORD.

1. Watch ye and wait, O breth-ren of God, Wait for the com-ing of Je-sus our Lord, A-ges have passed, yet bright grows the dawn, Je-sus has prom-ised to come in the morn.
2. Stead-fast-ly wait, and pa-tient-ly pray, Thus did our fath-ers who "wished for the day;" Cheer-ful they toiled and calm-ly did die, Wait-ing for Je-sus to come from the sky.
3. Some day the sky will part like a scroll, O-ver the earth will the Judgement trump roll; But to the saints 'twill hap-pi-ness bring, Since they have wait-ed so long for their King.

CHORUS.

Wait! wait! Jesus will come, Soon will our Bridegroom descend from His throne; Wait! wait! Jesus will come, Je-sus is com-ing a-gain to His own.

Copyright, 1892, by E. S. Ufford. By per.

I Have It in My Soul, Hallelujah! 179

Dedicated to my friend, William P. Pratt, Portland, Maine.

E. S. U.   Rev. E. S. UFFORD.

1. Come, weep just as we did in sor-row for sin, Come, knock till the Lord bid you en-ter within; Come trust-ing, ex-pecting, There's no oth-er way, And soon you will find it the gladsome new day.
2. Come, pray just as we did to live hour by hour, Above earth's temptations, with God's keeping pow'r; To kneel oft in prayer is vic-t'ry be-gun, Thus wrestling with e-vil the crown will be won.
3. Come, shout just as we did your "Glo-ry to God!" Sing prais-es to Je-sus, who saves by His blood; The song of re-demption shall be our re-frain, Till in the new heaven we sing it a-gain.

CHORUS.

I have it in my soul, hal-le-lu-jah! I have found the Savior precious all the way, all the way, I was once a child of sin, but I let my Savior in, And there's sunlight in my soul to-day.

Copyright, 1894, by E. S. Ufford.

Hear Ye Not the Savior.

Come unto me, all ye that labor and are heavy laden, and I will give you rest."—Matt. 11: 28.

C. W. R. C. W. RAY.

1. Hear ye not the Sav-ior call - ing, Gent-ly call - ing aft - er thee?
2. In the sweetest ac cents plead-ing, Pointing to the blood-y tree;
3. Art thou still thy need de - bat - ing, Canst thou not thy dan-ger see?

On thine ear His voice is fall - ing; Come, poor sinner, "Come to Me."
Where for thee He once hung bleeding, Still He whispers, "Come to Me."
Wouldst thou lon-ger keep Him wait-ing, Sad-ly pleading, "Come to Me."

REFRAIN.

Ten - der - ly He doth en-treat thee; Pa-tient - ly He waits to greet thee:

rit.

If in judgement He shall meet thee, Fearful then shall be thy doom.

Copyright, 1894, by C. W. Ray.

186. Sabbath Day Song.

B. W. Camp. J. H. Alleman.

1. O beau-ti-ful day, bright Sab-bath day That Jesus hath giv'n for rest, His word let us search for truths that we may By faith in His promise be blest.
2. Our la-bors and cares we'll lay a-side, Our hearts un-to Him we'll bring; We'll turn from the world, its fol-lies de-ride, To honor the Sav-ior, our King.
3. We'll sing of the day, dear Sab-bath day That Jesus, the Lord hath blest; From earth and its cares we're pass-ing a-way To en-ter the Sab-bath of rest.

CHORUS.

We'll sing of the beau-ti-ful Sab-bath day, The day of all oth-ers the best, 'Till Jesus shall call His dear children a-way To en-ter the Sab-bath of rest.

Used by per. of J. H. Alleman, Publisher, Chicago, Ill.

Papa, Shall I Look For You?

Dedicated to the memory of AMY GRACE BEABLE.

For more than two years this child of Jesus, only nine years of age, had vainly besought her father to come to the Savior. Sickness at last seized her, and death came; but before the spirit took its flight she gave expression to these beautiful words, "I am going up; come, hurry up, mamma,—tell papa to come." Then, speaking to others, she said, "Won't *you* come?" Then, to her father, who had just arrived, she said, "Papa, come!" "I will come," said the father, "I can't have my child in heaven and not be there too."

Words and Music by J. W. VAN DE VENTER.

1. I am go-ing up, dear pa-pa, Are you coming by and by?
2. Won't you promise me, dear pa-pa? Je - sus wants you there, I know.
3. Yes, I'll come, my lit - tle darling, Calm your fears and doubt no more;
4. She has passed be-yond the riv-er, And we hear her voice no more;

Won't you come to see your darling In the home be-yond the sky?
Will you meet me up in heaven? Tell me now, be-fore I go.
I will meet my child in heaven, When this drea - ry life is o'er.
She is rest-ing, sweet-ly rest-ing, O - ver on the oth - er shore;

At the gate-way I'll be waiting When the lov - ing ones pass thro';
At the gate-way I'll be waiting When the lov - ing ones pass thro';
Tell the Sav - ior I am coming, That He saves your pa - pa, too;
But the Sav - ior is in - vit-ing, And the call is ev - er new:

I will see them as they en - ter; Pa-pa, shall I look for you?
I will see them as they en - ter; Pa-pa, shall I look for you?
Thro' His bless-ed love and mer - cy, By and by I'll be with you.
Will you hear the in - vi - ta - tion? Sinner, He is call-ing you!

Copyright, 1894, by J. W. Van De Venter.

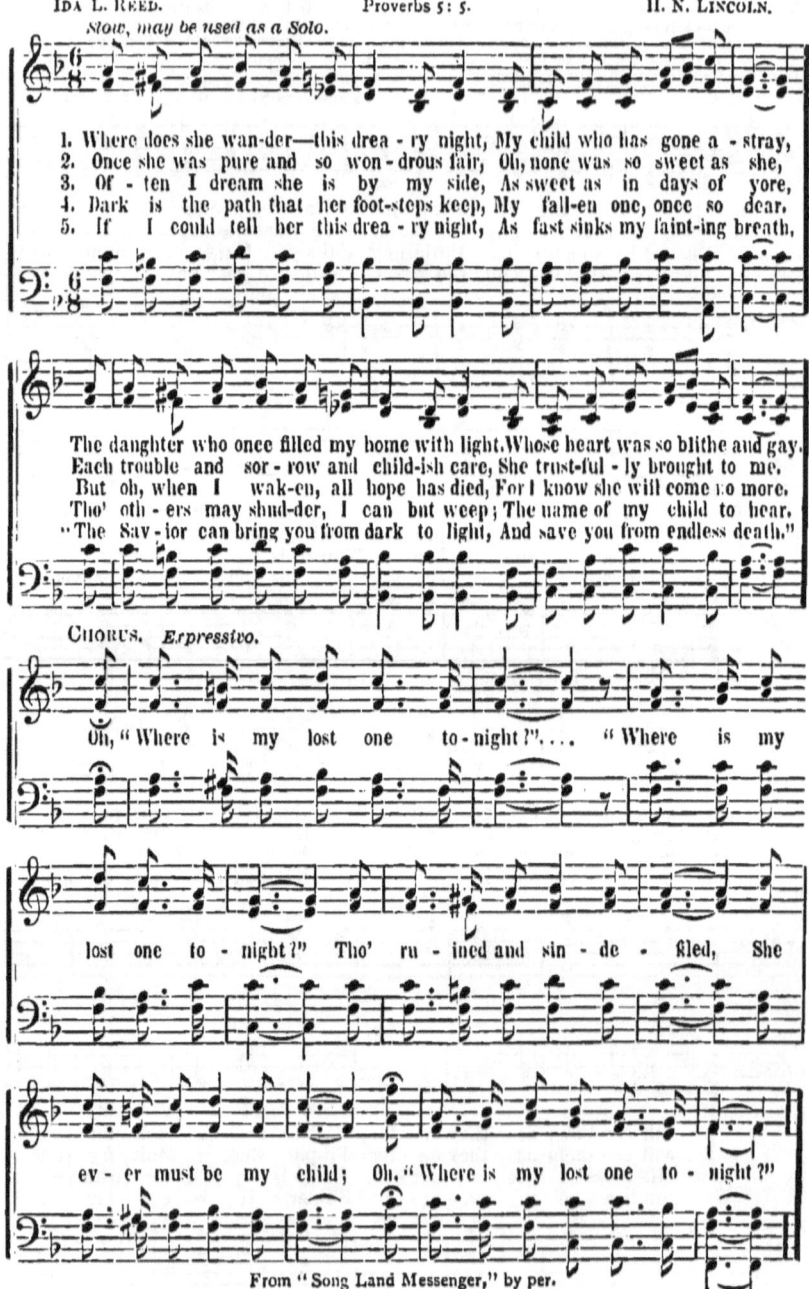

The Sinner and the Song.

By WILL L. THOMPSON.

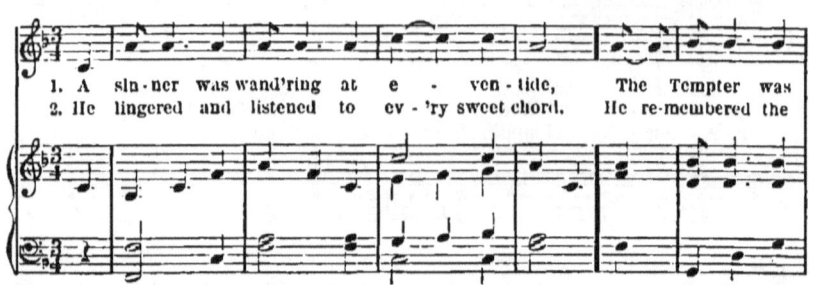

1. A sinner was wand'ring at eventide, The Tempter was
2. He lingered and listened to ev'ry sweet chord, He remembered the

watching close by at his side, In his heart raged a battle for
time he once loved the Lord. Come on! says the Tempter, come

right against wrong. But, hark! from the church he hears the sweet song:
on with the throng, But, hark! from the church again swells the song:

QUARTET, to be sung very softly.

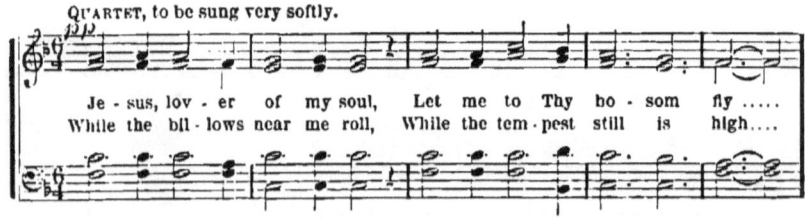

Jesus, lover of my soul, Let me to Thy bosom fly
While the billows near me roll, While the tempest still is high

From "Thompson's Popular Anthems," Copyrighted and Published by
Will L. Thompson, East Liverpool, Ohio.

Sowing and Reaping. Concluded.

o'er;.... If we sow........ the seeds of love.... God will
days are o'er; If we sow seeds of love,

take.... us home a-bove,.... If we sow the seeds of love.
God will take, home a-bove.

Waseca.

LEONARD WEAVER, Evangelist.　　　　　　　　W. S. WEEDEN.

1. Lead Thou me on, O Lord, 'twill be e-nough If Thou art with me,
2. Lead Thou me on, O Lord, leave not a-lone Amidst the dark-ness
3. Lead Thou me on, for Thou art all I need, When hungry Thou the

tho' the road be rough; Thy presence will sup-ply me peace and rest,
of this world Thine own; But guide me, as a shepherd, all the way,
bread of life canst feed; If faint or thirst-y, Thou, the liv-ing spring,

And calm all anxious throbbings of the breast.
And hold me ev-er near Thee, lest I stray.
Canst sweet re-freshment to my spir-it bring.

4.
Lead Thou me on, O Lord,
  and all is light;
What can I ask for more by
  day or night?
'Twill be enough if but Thy
  face I see,
And feel Thine own strong
  hand is leading me.

Copyright, 1894, by W. S. Weeden.

The Prodigal Daughter.

TALLIE MORGAN.

Slow, with expression.

1. To the home of the fath-er re - turn-ing, The prod - i - gal,
2. But ah! for the prod - i - gal daughter, Who has wan-dered a -
3. But thanks to the Shepherd whose mercy, Still fol - lows the

wea - ry and worn, Is greet-ed with joy and thanksgiving, As
- way from her home, Her feet must still press the dark val - ley, And
sheep tho' they stray. The weak-est and e'en the for - sak - en, He

rit.   a tempo.

when on his first natal morn. A robe and a ring is his por - tion,
thro' the wild wilderness roam. A-lone on the bleak barren mountains,
bears on His bosom a - way. And in the bright mansions of glo - ry,

The servants as sup-pli - ants bow, He is clad in fine lin-en and
The mountain so dreary and cold, No hand is outstretched in fond
Which the blood of His sacri-fice won, There is room for the prodigal

pur - ple, In re-turn for his pen - i - tent vow, He is clad in fine
pi - ty, To welcome her back to the fold, No hand is out -
daughter, As well as the prod-i - gal son, There is room for the

Copyright, 1894, by Tallie Morgan.

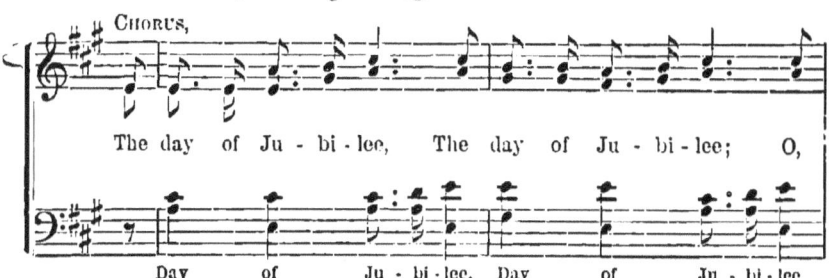

198. Give Him a Cheer.

At a tenement-house fire in New York City, the throngs of people saw, through flames and smoke, a young woman in her night-robe at a fifth story window, clinging to the window-casing, while her gaze was fixed on the excited people below. The fire-ladder was too short to reach the window; but a brave fireman made a desperate effort to go up the ladder, through the flames, to a point from which the young woman could spring into his arms. When half way up the ladder, as a fresh burst of flame shot about, the fireman seemed to falter and began to retrace his steps. At this critical moment a man in the crowd shouted out, "*For God's sake—give him a cheer!*" which was done with tremendous power. He immediately made a desperate rush through flame and smoke, where the imperiled young woman sprang into his arms, and he brought her safely to the ground.

A. C. F.   (May be sung as a Solo or Duet, with Refrain.)   Rev. A. C. Ferguson.

1. There's a tried, struggling heart, half hop-ing to win A tri-umph o'er trouble, or sorrow, or sin; The wild, lu-rid flames leap a-bout where he stands—We may give him heart-cheer, we may give him our hands.
2. How lit-tle we know of the longings within The sin-burdened souls that e'en now would be-gin To turn from the vile, for the pure and the true. If helped just in time, tho' our deeds are but few.
3. Sin's fires, so vast, are rag-ing around, While poor, blistered hearts lie prone on the ground; The hiss of the flames is heard in the street; Shall we bind up the wounds of the sad ones we meet?
4. How glorious the work! 'Tis for you and for me To point the dimm'd eyes lov-ing Je-sus to see; Thus, see-ing by faith 'twas for them that He came, the form of "*The Fourth*" they'll behold 'mid the flame.

Refrain. *Spirited.*

Go, give him a cheer! O, give him a cheer! Who yet may have

Copyright, 1894 by A. C. Ferguson.

Give Him a Cheer. Concluded.

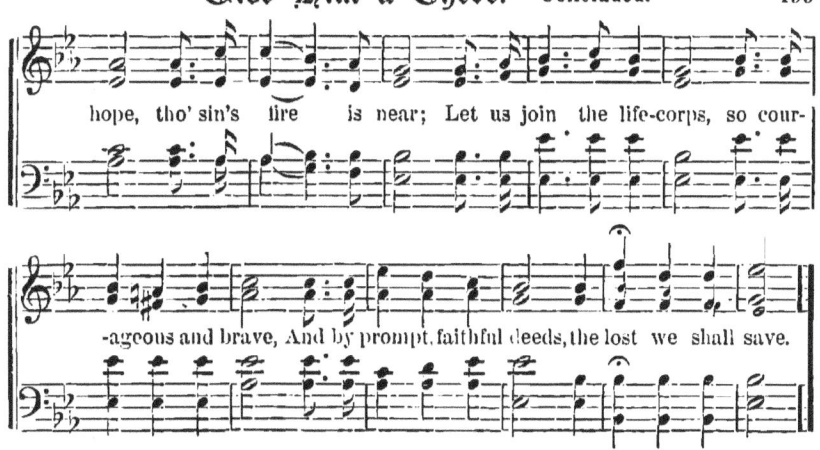

hope, tho' sin's fire is near; Let us join the life-corps, so cour-ageous and brave, And by prompt, faithful deeds, the lost we shall save.

The Fountain Now is Open.

Rev. Jos. Hart, 1759. Arr. by J. W. Van De Venter.

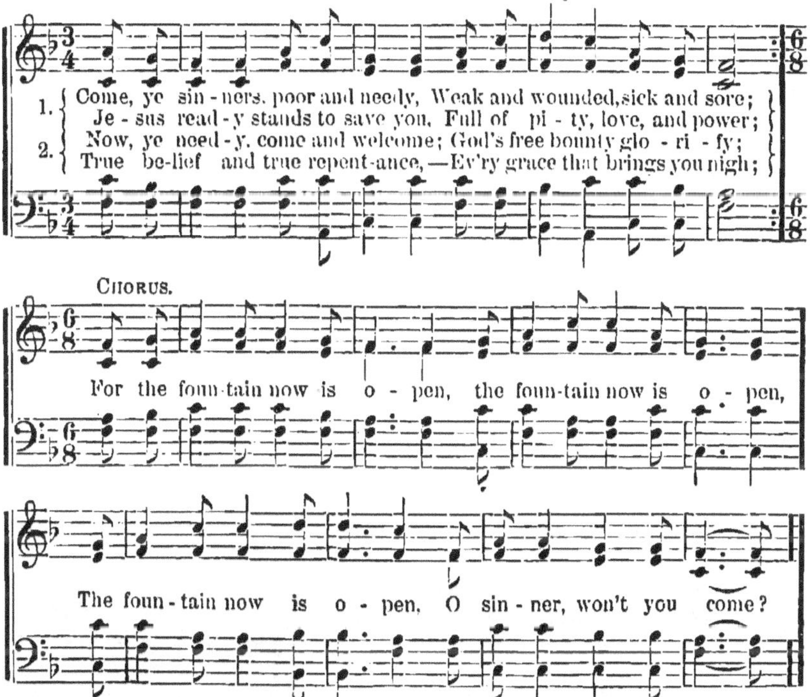

1. Come, ye sin-ners, poor and needy, Weak and wounded, sick and sore;
   Je-sus read-y stands to save you, Full of pi-ty, love, and power;
2. Now, ye need-y, come and welcome; God's free bounty glo-ri-fy;
   True be-lief and true repent-ance,—Ev'ry grace that brings you nigh;

CHORUS.

For the foun-tain now is o-pen, the foun-tain now is o-pen, The foun-tain now is o-pen, O sin-ner, won't you come?

3 Let not conscience make you linger;
   Nor of fitness fondly dream;
   All the fitness He requireth
   Is to feel your need of Him;

4 Come, ye weary, heavy-laden,
   Bruised and mangled by the fall;
   If you tarry till you're better,
   You will never come at all;

Copyright, 1894, by J. W. Van De Venter.

Raise the Song Triumphant.

Play first four measures for prelude. Words and music by GEO. NOYES ROCKWELL.

VOICES IN UNISON. *Spirited.*

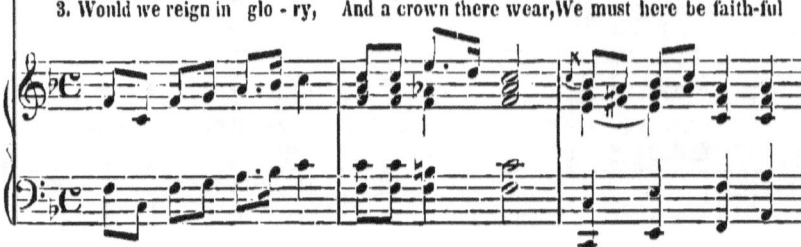

1. Raise the song tri-umph-ant, Sing in cho-rus strong; Let all earth re-ech-o
2. Tho' sin and temp-ta-tion Ev-'rywhere abound, Tho' the hosts of Sa-tan
3. Would we reign in glo-ry, And a crown there wear, We must here be faith-ful

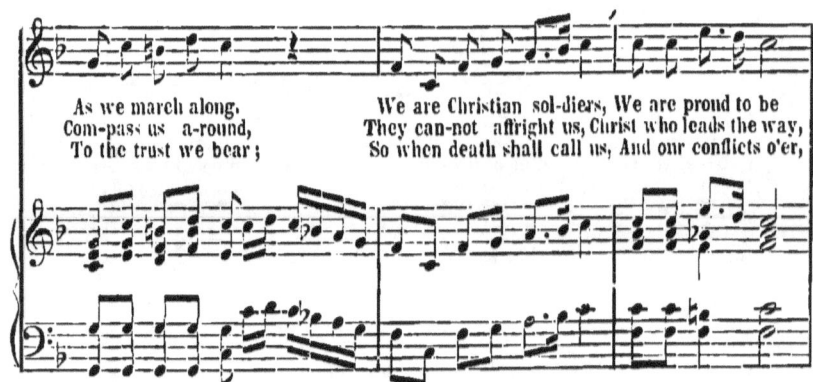

As we march along, We are Christian sol-diers, We are proud to be
Com-pass us a-round, They can-not affright us, Christ who leads the way,
To the trust we bear; So when death shall call us, And our conflicts o'er,

CHORUS.

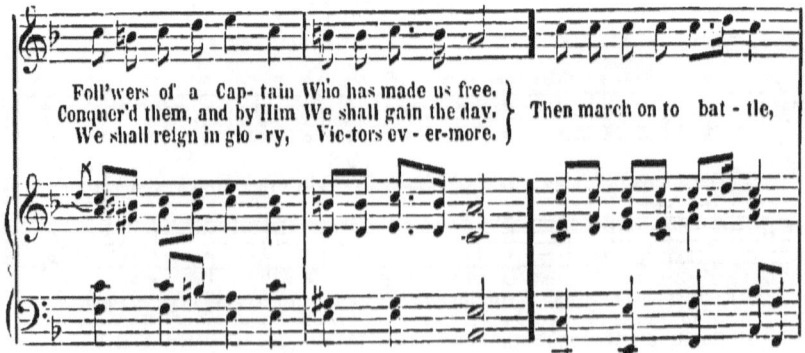

Foll'wers of a Cap-tain Who has made us free.
Conquer'd them, and by Him We shall gain the day. } Then march on to bat-tle,
We shall reign in glo-ry, Vic-tors ev-er-more.

From "Songs of Y. W. C. Temperance Union," by per.

I Am Trusting in My Savior.

205

LEONARD WEAVER, Evangelist.   J. W. WARD.

1. I am trusting in my Sav-ior, For his death up-on the tree;
2. I am looking un-to Je-sus, To sup-ply all dai-ly grace;

Has re-moved all condem-na-tion, And from sin has set me free.
And so sweet-ly I am rest-ing In the sun-shine of His face.

CHORUS.

Rest-ing so sweet-ly, Fol-low-ing so close-ly,
Kept for His ser-vice I e'er would be Wait-ing and watching,
Work-ing and prais-ing 'Till in the glo-ry His face I see.

3 I am living now to serve Him,
   Go or wait at His command;
   Like a servant, ever ready
   To obey I listening stand.

4 I am working for the Master
   In the harvest field to-day;
   Oh, how sweet it is to follow,
   When His Spirit leads the way.

5 I am following in the foot-prints
   He has left along the way;
   And, tho' rough at times the journey,
   Yet it leads to endless day.

6 I am waiting for His coming,
   When the working day is o'er;
   I am watching and I'm longing,
   To be with Him evermore.

Copyright, 1894, by W. S. Weeden.

The Better Land. Concluded.

REFRAIN.

That bet-ter land, where an-gels stand,
That bet-ter land, where an-gels stand.
And sing His prais-es o'er; I'm go-ing there,
I'm going there,
His joy to share, And live for-ev-er-more.
His joy to share,

Gloria Patri.

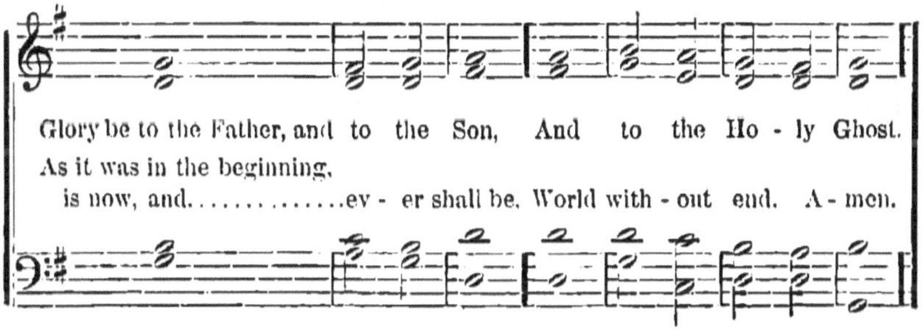

Glory be to the Father, and to the Son, And to the Ho-ly Ghost.
As it was in the beginning,
is now, and............ev-er shall be, World with-out end. A-men.

208. Draw Near, Fair Eden.

J. W. Van De Venter.   W. S. Weeden.

1. We lay our dear ones down to rest, And wipe away a fall-ing tear, Then turn our eyes to yon-der shore, And fan-cy it is drawing near: We see their fac-es in the throng, The lov-ing smile, the wav-ing hand; We catch the mel-o-dy of song, And long to fly to yon bright land.

2. The time to wait will not be long, Tho' dreary years may roll between: Each mo-ment brings us near-er home And adds new beau-ty to the scene; The sore af-flic-tions we endure, The heav-y loads we have to bear, The hours of sor-row we pass through Secures for us our treasure there.

CHORUS.

Draw near, fair E-den, ve-ry near, And hov-er o'er this world of care;

Copyright, 1894, by W. S. Weeden.

Farewell.

J. W. Van De Venter. J. Kinkle. Arr. by G. B.

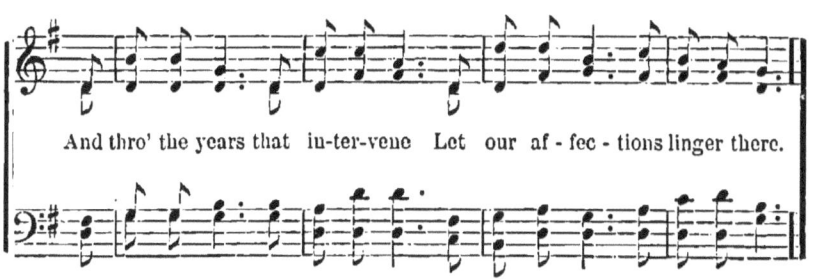

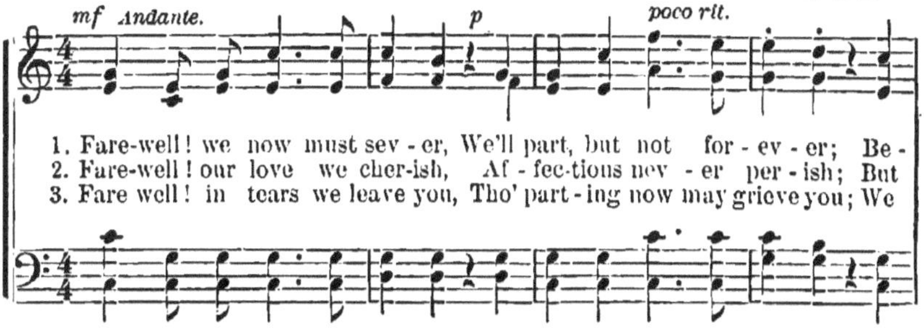

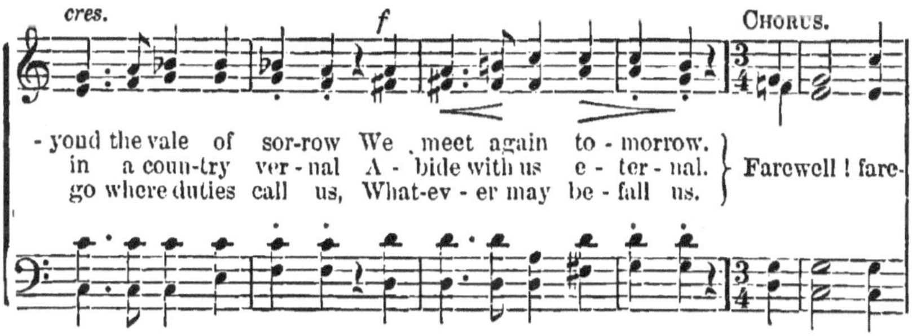

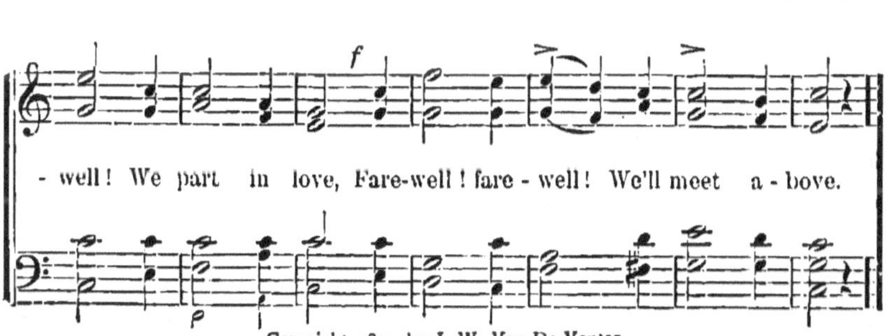

They are Covered by the Blood. 213

L. E. JONES.
I. H. MEREDITH.

1. I brought my sins to Cal-va-ry, They are cov-ered by the blood of Je-sus; There He in mer-cy set me free, They are
2. My woes are bur-ied 'neath the tide, They are cov-ered by the blood of Je-sus; Be-neath the foun-tain deep and wide, They are
3. 'Twas my trans-gres-sions that He bore, They are cov-ered by the blood of Je-sus; Now He re-mem-bers them no more, They are
4. The bur-dens that my soul op-prest, They are cov-ered by the blood of Je-sus; He took them all and gave me rest, They are

CHORUS.

cov-ered by the blood of Je - sus, They are cov-ered by the blood, cov-ered by the blood, Cov-ered by the blood of Je - sus; Tho' crim-son were my sins I know, They are covered by the blood of Je - sus.

Copyright, 1894, by I. H. Meredith.

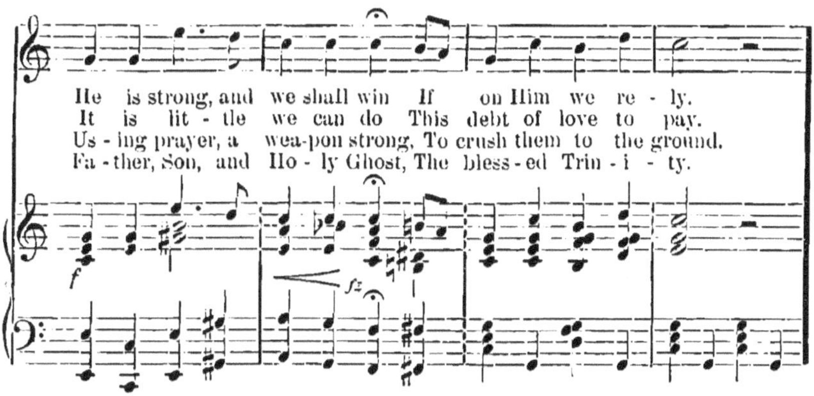

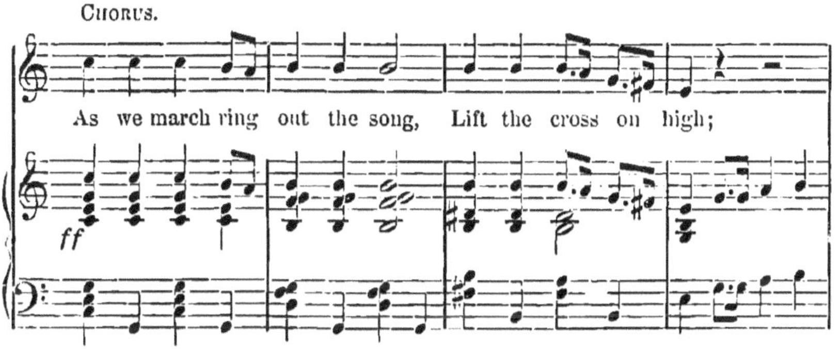

We are Soldiers of the Cross. Concluded. 217

He is strong, and we shall win If on Him we re - ly.
It is lit - tle we can do This debt of love to pay.
Us - ing prayer, a wea-pon strong, To crush them to the ground.
Fa - ther, Son, and Ho - ly Ghost, The bless - ed Trin - i - ty.

CHORUS.

As we march'ring out the song, Lift the cross on high;

Blow the trum-pet loud and long, And shout the bat-tle cry.

Angels Hovering Round.

1 There are angels hov'ring round, etc.
2 To carry the tidings home, etc.
3 To the New Jerusalem, etc.
4 Poor sinners are coming home, etc.
5 And Jesus bids them come, etc.
6 There's glory all around, etc.

FAMILIAR HYMNS. 219

219 *I Gave My Life for Thee.*

1 I gave my life for thee,
  My precious blood I shed,
That thou might'st ransomed be,
  And quickened from the dead.
‖: I gave, I gave my life for thee, :‖
  What hast thou given for Me?

2 My Father's house of light
  My glory-circled throne,
I left, for earthly night,
  For wand'rings sad and lone.
‖: I left, I left it all for thee, :‖
  Hast thou left aught for Me?

3 I suffered much for thee,
  More than thy tongue can tell,
Of bitterest agony,
  To rescue thee from hell.
‖: I've borne, I've borne it all for thee, :‖
  What hast thou borne for Me?

4 And I have brought to thee,
  Down from My home above,
Salvation full and free,
  My pardon and My love.
‖: I bring, I bring, rich gifts to thee, :‖
  What hast thou brought to Me?

220 *Haste, O Sinner, Now be Wise.*

1 Haste, O sinner, now be wise;
  Stay not for the morrow's sun:
Wisdom if you still despise
  Harder is it to be won.

2 Haste, and mercy now implore;
  Stay not for the morrow's sun,
Lest thy season shall be o'er
  Ere this evening's stage be run.

3 Haste, O sinner, now return,
  Stay not for the morrow's sun,
Lest thy lamp should cease to burn
  Ere salvation's work is done.

221 *Stand up for Jesus.*

1 Stand up, stand up for Jesus!
  Ye soldiers of the cross:
Lift high His royal banner,
  It must not suffer loss.
From vict'ry unto vict'ry
  His army shall He lead,
Till ev'ry foe is vanquished,
  And Christ is Lord indeed.

2 Stand up, stand up for Jesus!
  The trumpet call obey:
Forth to the mighty conflict,
  In this His glorious day:
"Ye that are men now serve Him,"
  Against unnumbered foes;
Let courage rise with danger,
  And strength to strength oppose.

3 Stand up, stand up for Jesus!
  Stand in His strength alone;
The arm of flesh will fail you—
  Ye dare not trust your own:
Put on the gospel armor,
  And, watching unto prayer,
Where duty calls, or danger,
  Be never wanting there.

222 *Even Me.*

1 Lord, I hear of showers of blessing
  Thou art scattering full and free—
Show'rs the thirsty land refreshing;
  Let some droppings fall on me—
    Even me, even me,
  Let Thy blessing fall on me.

2 Pass me not, O gracious Father,
  Sinful tho' my heart may be;
Thou might'st leave me, but the rather
  Let Thy mercy fall on me—
    Even me, even me,
  Let Thy mercy fall on me.

3 Pass me not, O tender Savior!
  Let me love and cling to Thee;
I am longing for Thy favor,
  Whilst Thou art calling, oh, call me—
    Even me, even me,
  Let Thy blessing fall on me.

4 Pass me not, O mighty Spirit!
  Thou canst make the blind to see;
Witnesser of Jesus' merit,
  Speak the word of pow'r to me—
    Even me, even me,
  Let Thy blessing fall on me.

223 *And Can It Be?*

1 And can it be that I should gain
  An interest in the Savior's blood?
Died He for me, who caused His pain?
  For me, who Him to death pursued?
Amazing love! how can it be
That Thou, my Lord, shouldst die for me!

2 He left the Father's throne above,—
  So free, so infinite His grace!—
Emptied Himself of all but love,
  And bled for Adam's helpless race!
'Tis mercy all, immense and free,
For, O my God, it found out me!

3 Long my imprisoned spirit lay,
  Fast bound in sin and nature's night;
Thine eye diffused a quickening ray,
  I woke, the dungeon flamed with light:
My chains fell off, my heart was free,
I rose, went forth, and followed Thee,

224 Revive Us Again.

1 We praise Thee, O God! for the Son of
    Thy love,
For Jesus who died, and is now gone above.

Cho.—Hallelujah! Thine the glory,
      Hallelujah! amen;
      Hallelujah! Thine the glory,
      Revive us again.

2 We praise Thee, O God! for Thy Spirit
    of light,   [tered our night.
Who has shown us our Savior, and scat-

3 All glory and praise to the Lamb that
    was slain,   [cleansed every stain.
Who has borne all our sins, and hath

4 All glory and praise to the God of all
    grace,   [guided our ways.
Who has bought us, and sought us, and

5 Revive us again; fill each heart with
    Thy love;   [above.
May each soul be rekindled with fire from

225 There is a Fountain.

1 There is a fountain filled with blood,
    Drawn from Immanuel's veins;
And sinners plunged beneath that flood,
    Lose all their guilty stains.

2 The dying thief rejoiced to see
    That fountain in his day;
And there may I, though vile as he,
    Wash all my sins away.

3 Dear dying Lamb, Thy precious blood
    Shall never lose its power,
Till all the ransomed church of God
    Be saved to sin no more.

4 E'er since, by faith, I saw the stream
    Thy flowing wounds supply,
Redeeming love has been my theme,
    And shall be till I die.

5 Then in a nobler, sweeter song,
    I'll sing Thy power to save, [tongue
When this poor lisping, stammering
    Lies silent in the grave.

226 Sinners, Turn, Why will Ye Die?

1 Sinners, turn, why will ye die?
    God, your Maker, asks you why;
God, who did your being give,
    Made you with Himself to live.

2 Sinners, turn, why will ye die?
    God, your Savior, asks you why;
Will ye not in Him believe?
    He has died that you might live.

3 Sinners, turn, why will ye die?
    God, the Spirit, asks you why;
Often with you has He strove,
    Wooed you to embrace His love.

227 Take My Life and Let It Be.

1 Take my life and let it be
    Consecrated, Lord, to Thee;
Take my hands and let them move
    At the impulse of Thy love.

2 Take my feet and let them be
    Swift and beautiful for Thee;
Take my voice and let me sing
    Always—only—for my King.

3 Take my lips and let them be
    Fill'd with messages from Thee;
Take my silver and my gold,
    Not a mite would I withhold,

4 Take my moments and my days,
    Let them flow in endless praise;
Take my intellect and use
    Ev'ry pow'r as Thou shalt choose.

228 Just as I Am.

1 Just as I am, without one plea,
    But that Thy blood was shed for me,
And that Thou bidd'st me come to Thee,
    O Lamb of God! I come, I come!

2 Just as I am, and waiting not
    To rid my soul of one dark blot, [spot,
To Thee, whose blood can cleanse each
    O Lamb of God! I come, I come!

3 Just as I am, though toss'd about
    With many a conflict, many a doubt,
Fightings and fears within, without,
    O Lamb of God! I come, I come!

4 Just as I am, poor, wretched, blind,
    Sight, riches, healing of the mind,
Yea, all I need, in Thee to find,
    O Lamb of God! I come, I come!

5 Just as I am; Thou wilt receive,
    Wilt welcome, pardon, cleanse, relieve,
Because Thy promise I believe,
    O Lamb of God! I come, I come!

229 Blest be the Tie.

1 Blest be the tie that binds
    Our hearts in Christian love;
The fellowship of kindred minds
    Is like to that above.

2 Before our Father's throne,
    We pour our ardent prayers;
Our fears, our hopes, our aims are one,
    Our comforts, and our cares.

3 We share our mutual woes;
    Our mutual burdens bear;
And often for each other flows
    The sympathizing tear.

4 When we asunder part,
    It gives us inward pain;
But we shall still be join'd in heart,
    And hope to meet again.

230   *I Do Believe.*

1 Father, I stretch my hands to Thee,
   No other help I know;
   If Thou withdraw Thyself from me,
   Ah, whither shall I go?

Cho.—I do believe, I now believe,
    That Jesus died for me; [blood,
    And thro' His blood, His precious
   I shall from sin be free.

2 What did Thine only Son endure
   Before I drew my breath ;
   What pain, what labor to secure
   My soul from endless death!

3 O Jesus, could I this believe,
   I now should feel Thy power ;
   And all my wants Thou wouldst relieve
   In this accepted hour.

4 Author of faith, to Thee I lift
   My weary, longing eyes ;
   O, let me now receive that gift ;
   My soul without it dies.

231   *He is Calling.*

1 There's a wideness in God's mercy,
   Like the wideness of the sea:
   There's a kindness in His justice
   Which is more than liberty.

Cho.—He is calling, "Come to Me!"
   Lord, I gladly haste to Thee.

2 There is welcome for the sinner,
   And more graces for the good ;
   There is mercy with the Savior,
   There is healing in His blood.

3 For the love of God is broader
   Than the measure of man's mind;
   And the heart of the Eternal
   Is most wonderfully kind,

4 If our love were but more simple,
   We should take Him at His word,
   And our lives would be all sunshine
   In the sweetness of our Lord.

232   *Oh, How I Love Jesus!*

1 How sweet the name of Jesus sounds
   In a believer's ear!
   It soothes his sorrows, heals his wounds,
   And drives away his fear.

Cho.—||: Oh, how I love Jesus!:||
    Because He first loved me ;
   ||: How can I forget Thee!:||
    Dear Lord, remember me.

2 It makes the wounded spirit whole,
   And calms the troubled breast;
   'Tis manna to the hungry soul,
   And to the weary rest.

3 I would Thy boundless love proclaim
   With every fleeting breath;
   So shall the music of Thy name
   Refresh my soul in death.

233   *O Happy Day.*

1 O happy day that fix'd my choice
   On Thee, my Savior and my God!
   Well may this glowing heart rejoice,
   And tell its raptures all abroad.

Cho.—Happy day, happy day,
   When Jesus washed my sins away!
   He taught me how to watch and pray,
   And live rejoicing every day.
   Happy day, happy day,
   When Jesus washed my sins away.

2 O happy bond, that seals my vows
   To Him that merits all my love!
   Let cheerful anthems fill His house,
   While to that sacred shrine I move.

3 'Tis done ! the great transaction's done!
   I am my Lord's, and He is mine:
   He drew me, and I followed on,
   Charmed to confess the voice divine.

4 Now rest, my long-divided heart ;
   Fix'd on this blissful centre, rest ;
   Nor ever from thy Lord depart ;
   With Him of ev'ry good possess'd,

5 High Heaven that heard the solemn vow,
   That vow renew'd shall daily hear,
   Till in life's latest hour I bow,
   And bless in death a bond so dear.

234   *At the Fountain.*

1 Of Him who did salvation bring,
   I'm at the fountain drinking,
   I could forever think and sing,
   I'm on my journey home.

Cho.—Glory to God,
   I'm at the fountain drinking;
   Glory to God,
   I'm on my journey home

2 Ask but His grace, and lo ! 'tis giv'n,
   Ask and He turns your hell to heav'n.

3 Though sin and sorrow wound my soul,
   Jesus, thy balm will make me whole.

4 Where'er I am, where'er I move,
   I meet the object of my love.

5 Insatiate to this spring I fly,
   I drink and yet am ever dry.

Cho.—Glory to God,
   I'm at the fountain, drinking,
   Glory to God,
   My soul satisfied.

FAMILIAR HYMNS.

235   *Glorying in the Cross.*

1 When I survey the wondrous cross
   On which the Prince of Glory died,
My richest gain I count but loss,
   And pour contempt on all my pride.

2 Forbid it, Lord, that I should boast,
   Save in the death of Christ, my God,
All the vain things that charm me most,
   I sacrifice them to His blood.

3 See, from His head, His hands, His feet,
   Sorrow and love flow mingled down;
Did e'er such love and sorrow meet,
   Or thorns compose so rich a crown?

4 Were the whole realm of nature mine,
   That were a present far too small:
Love so amazing, so divine,
   Demands my soul, my life, my all.

236   *Arise, My Soul, Arise.*

1 Arise, my soul, arise;
   Shake off thy guilty fears;
The bleeding Sacrifice
   In my behalf appears.
‖: Before the throne my Surety stands;:‖
My name is written on His hands.

2 He ever lives above,
   For me to intercede,
His all-redeeming love,
   His precious blood to plead.
‖: His blood atoned for all our race,:‖
And sprinkles now the throne of grace.

3 To God I'm reconciled;
   His pardoning voice I hear;
He owns me for His child;
   I can no longer fear.
‖: With confidence I now draw nigh,:‖
And Father, Abba, Father, cry.

237   *Blow Ye the Trumpet, Blow.*

1 Blow ye the trumpet, blow,
   The gladly solemn sound;
Let all the nations know,
   To earth's remotest bound,
‖: The year of jubilee is come,:‖
Return, ye ransomed sinners, home.

2 Jesus, our great High Priest,
   Hath full atonement made;
Ye weary spirits, rest;
   Ye mournful souls, be glad;
‖: The year of jubilee is come;:‖
Return, ye ransomed sinners, home.

3 Extol the Lamb of God,—
   The all-atoning Lamb;
Redemption in His blood
   Throughout the world proclaim;
‖: The year of jubilee is come::‖
Return, ye ransomed sinners, home.

238   *Coronation.*

1 All hail the pow'r of Jesus' name!
   Let angels prostrate fall;
Bring forth the royal diadem,
   And crown Him Lord of all.

2 Let ev'ry kindred, ev'ry tribe,
   On this terrestrial ball,
To Him all majesty ascribe,
   And crown Him Lord of all.

3 Oh, that with yonder sacred throng
   We at His feet may fall;
We'll join the everlasting song,
   And crown Him Lord of all,

239   *My Faith Looks up to Thee.*

1 My faith looks up to Thee,
   Thou Lamb of Calvary,
     Savior divine;
Now hear me while I pray,
Take all my sins away;
Oh, let me from this day
     Be wholly Thine.

2 May Thy rich grace impart
Strength to my fainting heart,
     My zeal inspire;
As Thou hast died for me,
Oh, may my love to Thee
Pure, warm, and changeless be,
     A living fire.

3 When ends life's transient dream,
When death's cold, sullen stream
     Shall o'er me roll,
Blest Savior, then, in love,
Fear and distress remove;
Oh, bear me safe above,
     A ransomed soul!

240   *Must Jesus Bear the Cross?*

1 Must Jesus bear the cross alone,
   And all the world go free?
No, there's a cross for ev'ry one,
   And there's a cross for me.

2 The consecrated cross I'll bear
   Till death shall set me free;
And then go home my crown to wear,
   For there's a crown for me.

3 O precious cross! O glorious crown!
   O resurrection day!
Ye angels from the stars come down,
   And bear my soul away.

---

241   *Doxology.*

Praise God from whom all blessing flow;
Praise Him, all creatures here below;
Praise Him above, ye heavenly host;
Praise Father, Son, and Holy Ghost.

INDEX.

First lines in roman; Titles in CAPITALS; Metrical Tunes in *italic*.

A.

	No.
Adown life's vale we wa	141
A guilty sinner once was	20
A HAPPY BAND ARE WE,	105
A HARBOR OF REST, ...	66
A home on high is waiti	150
Ah! the wrongs that mi	166
Aldene, S. M.,	159
A LITTLE WHILE WITH J	164
All hail the power of Je	238
ALL THE WAY TO CALV	151
Almost persuaded, weary	69
ALREADY CONDEMNED,	180
Amazing grace, how sw	85
AMERICA! LAND OF THE	189
Am I a soldier of the cro	185
AN EVENING PRAYER,	21
And can it be that I shou	223
ANGELS HOV'RING ROU	217
An old soldier I stand w	42
Are you waiting for the c	12
Arise, my soul, arise,	236
Art thou weary, art thou	163
A SHELTER IN THE TIM	101
A sinner was wand'ring	190
As the Lord to Samuel sp	202
AT THE FOUNTAIN,	231
AWAKE! HE COMETH,	211

B.

	No.
BALM FOR ACHING HEA	138
BEGIN THE DAY WITH G	13
BE NOT AFRAID,	182
BLESSED BE HIS NAME,	119
Blest be the tie that bind	229
Blow ye the trumpet blo	237
BOYS' RECRUITING SONG,	132
BRIGHT HOME OF THE S	143
Burn ev'ry heart with qu	94

C.

	No.
CHEER FOR THE THIRST	102
CHRISTIAN, HOW CAN Y	18
CHRIST VICTORIOU'S	35
Clad in robes of spotless	122
CLIMBING ETERNITY'S S	156
Cling to the Mighty One,	99
COME, BROTHER, COME,	127
Come sing again the song	173
COME, SINNER, COME,	27
Come, sinners, to the gos	157
COME TO THE SAVIOR, 69,	157
Come, trembling sinner,	72
Come weal come woe, w	182
Come, weep just as we di	179
Come, ye sinners, poor a	199
CONSECRATION HYMN,	94
CORONATION,	238
CROWN HIM,	106

D.

	No.
DARE TO SAY NO,	152
DAY BY DAY,	167
Dear Lord, increase my	218
Dear mother, look back	74
Don't you hear the cry o	134
Down at the cross the S	34
DOWN IN THE LICENSED	110

	No.
Do you remember the de	111
Doxology,	241
DRAW NEAR, FAIR EDE	208

E.

	No.
EARNESTLY PRAY	81
Earth's physicians know	29
Elmhurst, L. M.,	131
EVEN ME,	222

F.

	No.
FALL INTO LINE, BOYS,	78
Fall in! ye soldiers of th	196
FAREWELL,	209
Father, I stretch my han	230
FIGHTING UNDERNEATH	168
For the blessed source of	50
FOR YOU AND FOR ME,	6
From ceaseless toil and p	92
From the highways and	158

G.

	No.
Gently evening bendeth,	137
GIVE HIM A CHEER,	198
Give thanks, all ye peop	89
Gloria Patri,	207
Glory be to the Father,	207
GLORYING IN THE CROSS,	235
GLORY TO THE BLEEDIN	173
God always deals in love	159
God so loved the world	180
GOOD NEWS GONE TO CA	147
Go preach the gospel tidi	98
Gwendolen, 8,5,8,3,	163

H.

	No.
HALLELUJAH TO THE L	175
Hark! I hear a soft refra	80
Hark! I hear a warning	135
Hark, the voice of Jesus	70
Haste, O sinner, now be	220
Hast thou by burdens sor	59
Hast thou grieved in un	95
Have you ever heard the	140
HEAR YE NOT THE SAV	181
Hear your blessed Maste	56
He hath spoken, "Be st	3
HE IS CALLING,	231
HERE AM I,	202
HE SAVES TO THE UTTE	73
HE'S THE PRINCE OF P	3
HIDE ME,	112
HOLD UP THE LIGHT,	160
HOLY SPIRIT FROM ABO	10
Ho! my brother, hear th	132
How often in moments o	88
How sweet the name of	232
HOW THEY CRUCIFIED	43

I.

	No.
I am going up, dear Papa,	187
I AM TRUSTING IN MY SA	205
I am weak and heavy la	107
I brought my cares to Cal	213
I CAN, I WILL, I DO BEL	165
I DO BELIEVE	230
I follow the footsteps of	103
IF WE WOULD BUT SEE	166

	No.
I gave my life for thee,	219
I have a Shepherd, one I	68
I have found a Friend, o	175
I have found the great sa	119
I HAVE IT IN MY SOUL, II	179
I have wandered, deares	136
I HEARD THE VOICE OF	100
I hear the heavenly bell	63
I'LL GO TO JESUS,	72
I love to meditate, O Go	171
I'm glad I've got religio	147
I'M GOING HOME TO GLO	204
I'M GOING TO JESUS TO	125
I'm kneeling at the mer	165
I'M NOT AFRAID,	195
In a weather-worn old c	148
IN BEULAH LAND,	48
I NEED THEE, LORD,	145
In sympathy for those w	84
IN THE SECRET OF HIS	65
In the wilderness dreary,	124
INVOCATION,	215
IS IT FOR ME,	44
IS IT NOTHING TO YOU,	31
I stand; but not as once	176
I stand by the shore of a	33
I TELL HIM ALL,	9
IT WAS FOR ME,	38
I WILL SING OF THE ME	60

J.

	No.
Jesus, and shall it ever b	36
JESUS BIDS YOU COME,	55
JESUS IS CALLING NOW,	51
Jesus is calling, tenderly	104
JESUS IS MINE,	63
Jesus of Nazareth,	242
Jesus, see me at Thy fee	91
JESUS TENDERLY CALLI	101
JESUS THE RECONCILER,	15
JOHN, THREE, SIXTEEN,	203
JOY IN HEAVEN,	23
Just as I am, without on	228
JUST THE SAME TO-DAY,	140

K.

	No.
KEEP MOVING ON THE W	151

L.

	No.
LAY THY BURDEN DOW	59
Lead me, O Thou blesse	67
Lead Thou me on, O Lor	193
LESS OF SELF,	115
LET ME DIE AT MY POST,	42
LET IT SHINE,	170
Let the world have its di	214
Lift up your heads, ye pil	4
LISTEN TO MY STORY,	34
LITTLE THINGS,	58
LOOKING O'ER THE RIV	123
Lord, I hear of showers	222

M.

	No.
MAKE ROOM FOR JESUS,	61
MARCH ON,	142
May fainting souls appro	102
MERCY AT THE CROSS,	128
MERCY'S GATE,	37

(223)

INDEX.

	No.
MIGHTY TO SAVE	144
Must Jesus bear the cros	210
My country, 'tis of thee,	164
My faith looks up to Th	239
My heart is full of gladu	204
MY HEART'S PRAYER,	218
MY MOTHER'S SILV'RY H	74
MY SPIRIT IS FREE,	103

N.

	No.
Not an aching heart is ye	138
NOT ASHAMED OF JESUS,	36
NOTHING BUT THY BLO	91
Now be my heart inspire	131

O.

	No.
O beautiful day, bright S	186
O captive soul, why long	41
O church of Christ,	40
Of Him who did salvatio	234
Oft we tread the path be	192
O God, to-night I cannot	21
O God, Thou art the Kin	215
OH, ADMIT HIM,	56
O happy day that fixed	233
Oh, come, believe on Je	54
Oh, how dark the night	151
OH, HOW I LOVE JESUS,	232
OH! THAT I KNEW,	26
OH! THE BLOOD,	11
O mother, don't weep for	125
O mourner in Zion, how	79
On Calvary, despised, al	24
Once I was a lost one, a	203
ONLY A WORD,	17
Only looking o'er the riv	123
ONLY TOUCH HIM,	29
ONLY TRUST,	95
On the cross of Calvary	38
ONWARD UP THE HIGH	96
O sinner, take heed,	116
O, the cross of Jesus lift	117
O, there is a beautiful cit	177
Our blessed Redeemer ca	73
OUR COUNTRY'S VOICE,	162
Our Father, who art in	83
Our Hope is firm in Jesu	120
OUR LOVED ONES, OUR	62
Our sighs and tears	195
Out on the wide, wide oc	66
OVER ON THE BORDER L	150
O, WE'RE A LOYAL ARMY,	22

P.

	No.
PAPA, SHALL I LOOK FO	187
PASS OVER TO THY REST,	92
PHELPS,	20
Praise God from whom a	241
PRAISE YE THE LORD,	172
Precious Jesus, O, to lov	71
PRECIOUS TRUTH,	50
Precious Savior, we are	45
PREPARE TO MEET THY	135

R.

	No.
RAISE THE SONG TRIUM	200
REDEEMER OF ZION,	28
REMEMBER YOUR MOTH	210
REVIVE US AGAIN,	224
RING OUT, YE GOSPEL B	52
ROBES OF SPOTLESS WH	122
Rose of Sharon, thy rich	30

S.

	No.
SABBATH DAY SONG,	186
SAVED BY HIS BLOOD,	46
SAVIOR, KEEP ME NEAR	86
Savior, make me pure w	86
SCATTERING PRECIOUS S	93
SEND THE LIGHT,	130
SEND THE NEWS,	16
Sing, all ye ransomed of	142
Sinners, turn, why will y	226
Softly and tenderly Jesus	6
SOLDIER OF THE CROSS,	185
SOLDIERS OF THE KING,	146
SOLDIERS OF THE LORD,	90
SOMETIME,	178
SOMETIME THE VEIL WI	88
SONG OF PEACE,	126
SONG OF PRAISE,	89
SONGS THAT MOTHER SA	80
SOUGHT AND FOUND,	14
SOWING AND REAPING,	192
SPEAK KINDLY TO THE	7
Stand up, stand up for Je	221
STEP OUT ON THE PROM	79
SWEET ROSE OF SHARO	30
SWEET WORDS OF PEAC	183

T.

	No.
TAKE MY HAND, DEAR F	87
Take my life, and let it be,	227
THE BEAUTIFUL CITY,	177
THE BELIEVER'S STANDI	176
THE BETTER LAND,	206
THE CHRISTIAN'S HOPE,	120
THE CROSS OF CALVARY,	24
THE CROSS OF JESUS LIF	117
THE DAILY CROSS,	77
THE DAY OF JUBILEE,	196
The deed was done, the d	114
THE DYING BOATMAN,	148
THE FOUNTAIN NOW IS O	199
THE GRACE OF GOD,	32
THE HAVEN,	129
THE KINGDOM SHALL EN	108
THE KINGDOM TO COME,	214
THE KING'S HIGHWAY,	57
THE LORD IS MY SHEPH	68
THE LORD'S PRAYER,	83
THE MASTER IS CALLIN	70
THE MORNING COMETH,	4
THE OPEN TOMB,	114
THE PENITENT'S PRAYE	107
THE PHARISEE AND PU	82
THE PRODIGAL DAUGHT	194
There are angels hov'rin	217
There are thousands who	170
There is a better land ab	206
There is a city made of g	143
There is a fountain filled	225
THERE IS HOPE,	155
There is joy among the a	23
There is mercy at the cr	128
There is only one thing t	154
There's a call comes ring	130
There's a haven safely lo	129
There's a tried, struggli	198
There's a wideness in G	231
There went to the templ	82
The Savior called so lovi	46
THE SAVIOR'S CALL,	76

	No.
The Savior sought and f	11
THE SINNER AND THE SO	190
The sin-taint of earth is s	48
The soul who would find	61
The Spirit now entreatet	37
The storm sweeps over G	126
The voice that is calling	76
THE WANDERER'S RETU	136
THE WEDDING GARMEN	158
THE WONDERFUL STORY,	124
THEY ARE COVERED BY	213
They are safe in the harb	62
This life is beset with te	210
THROW OUT THE LINE,	134
Thy grace, O my Savior,	32
Till I learned to love Th	15
TIME'S RESTLESS TIDE,	141
TO ENTER HEAVEN'S GAT	139
To the home of the fathe	194
Trust in the Lord to hide	167
Two builders are at wor	39

U.

	No.
Up from the dark, gloom	156

W.

	No.
WAITING,	33
WAITING FOR HIS COMI	12
WAIT! WAIT! JESUS WI	174
Walking daily with the	35
Wake the strain, the gla	105
Wake, weary bride, from	211
Wardell,	167
Waseca,	193
Was it for me that Jesus	44
Watch ye and wait, O b	174
WE ARE SOLDIERS OF T	216
We are soldiers of the K	146
We are soldiers of the L	168
We are soldiers true and	90
WE ARE THINE,	45
Weeden, C.M.,	171
We have a rock, a safe r	101
We lay our dear ones do	208
WE'LL NEVER SAY GOOD	118
We pass along thro' toil	139
WE PRAISE THEE, O LO	97
We praise Thee, O Lord,	224
We're marching to Monn	57
WE SHALL GATHER AT T	64
We shall meet beyond th	64
We've enlisted in the ar	78
WHATEVER YOU SOW Y	116
WHAT I HAVE WRITTEN,	212
WHAT WILL YOU DO WI	8
When cherished joys ha	145
When I survey the won	235
When I think how they	43
When Jehovah pass'd in	11
When you see a mighty	58
Where does she wander	188
WHERE IS MY LOST ONE	188
Where is my wand'ring	110
WHERE WILL YOU SPEN	47
While Jesus whispers to	27
Who fain would follow	77
WHY LONGER WAIT,	41
WONDERFUL IS THE SAV	184

Y.

	No.
Yes, the sorrow, pain an	118
YES, WE'RE COMING,	54

PRESS AND PULPIT NOTICES.

I cannot possibly find words to adequately express the high appreciation in which I hold W. S. Weeden, as a musical director for Chautauqua Assemblies, as a soloist, and as a Christian gentleman. He is a magnificent singer, an inspiring director, a bright, sunshiny man of even temper, who can always be trusted to do the right thing, and to do it well.
REV. W. L. DAVIDSON, D.D., Supt. of Instruction.
Cuyahoga Falls, Ohio, Oct. 6, 1893.

W. S. Weeden is by all odds the best male soloist that has yet appeared before a Beatrice Chautauqua audience. His voice is a magnificent baritone.
The Daily Express (Beatrice, Neb., June, 1893).

That I am without musical capability—instrumental, I know ; vocal, my friends eagerly assure me. But I have a listening ear, and to the thorough and general esteem in which Mr. Weeden is held at Chautauqua Assemblies as a musical director, I gladly testify.
Cuba, New York, August 19, 1893. DEWITT MILLER, Lecturer.

One of the great attractions of the assembly has been the singing of Mr. Weeden, the chorus conductor. We should hardly know what to do without him. Mr. Weeden's forte is in assembly and chorus work, and in this he is said by his colleagues to have no equal at present in the country.
Times Republican (Marshalltown, Iowa, July 20, 1893).

Mr. W. S. Weeden sings to the heart with artistic grace and sweetness and is a skillful leader. REV. RUSSELL H. CONWELL.
Philadelphia, Pa., July 22, 1893.

This was Mr. Weeden's second Chautauqua appearance here. He is a fine chorus trainer and conductor. *Lexington Transcript* (July, 1893).

As a pastor, and especially as an assembly director for ten years, I have had much to do with musical directors, and in the list are some names known throughout the land. I do not hesitate to say that W. S Weeden easily excels all the others. He has the power of inspiring enthusiasm in his choruses, which insures the highest success in chorus work. As a soloist he is exceptional H. C. JENNINGS, Supt. Waseca Assembly.
Red Wing, Minn., Sept. 23, 1893.

W. S. Weeden is an ideal musical director. He is the possessor of a magnificent voice, which he uses with rare taste and expression in solo work ; while his fine presence, technical skill, enthusiastic devotion to his art, and sterling personal character make him an exceptionally strong and popular conductor E. C. WHALEN, Superintendent.
Spirit Lake, Iowa, July 26, 1893.

I know W. S. Weeden to be a thorough artist, as well as Christian gentleman. As a chorus organizer and conductor he is simply unrivaled—as a solo singer he is splendidly equipped with a glorious voice, artistic taste, and, best of all, tact and sense of fitness in his selections.
Harrisburg, Pa., Sept. 1, 1893. L. F. COPELAND, Lecturer.

W. S. Weeden has had many years of experience in conducting music at large assemblies all over the country. He will be pleased to correspond with committees who have need of such a man. He is perfectly at home in Chautauqua work, camp meetings, Young People's Society of Christian Endeavor and Epworth League Conventions, Young Men's Christian Association Conventions, Temperance Rallies, Evangelistic work, and all special meetings of the church. Address all communications to

W. S. WEEDEN, 106 WAVERLY PLACE, NEW YORK.

www.ingramcontent.com/pod-product-compliance
Lightning Source LLC
Chambersburg PA
CBHW022014220426
43663CB00007B/1080